MEMOIRS

by
William "Bill" Walls
May 14, 1933 – Feb. 2025

A Redneck Rebel's Travel from Rags to Tuxedo

GOD
FAMILY
COUNTRY

COPYRIGHT

Copyright © 2025 William Walls

Published by

All rights reserved. No part of this book may be reproduced or transmitted in any form or by any means, electronic or mechanical, including photocopying, recording, or by any information storage and retrieval system, without written permission from the publisher and author.

This is a Memoir. Some names, characters, businesses, places, events, and incidents in this book are true to the author's recollection of events contained. Some names and events are changed to protect privacy in a polite manner, but not so much to obfuscate the recollected facts and opinions.

ABOUT MY STORY

It is factual about my thirty years in poverty and almost sixty-two years with plenty but not abundance. It includes my life during the great depression; my education; my teaching and instructing.

It covers sixty-five years of international travel, twenty three of which were living overseas. I had a good relationship with US Military and local commanders and with foreign military officials. I had a close relationship with foreign generals, kings, knights, presidents, ministers, and ambassadors.

I was in caught in the middle of riots, demonstrations, in insurrections, assassinations, executions and the overthrow of governments.

I closely saw starvation, pestilences, cholera epidemics, mutilations, and worse things than most Americans can imagine, but I saw peace, tranquility and abundance in countries until US Foreign aid came. It was always mismanaged or not managed at all. The US president is at fault because of ambassadors that he selects and the US Aid programs that he tolerates. I saw perfect examples in Indonesia and Iran.

President Jimmy Carter was a good example of a bad president. He was reportedly a Christian and had plans to make the world a better place, but was ignorant and misadvised by the staff that he selected. He caused the governments of Iran, Angola, South Africa, Rhodesia, Sudan and other countries to be overthrown and fall to our enemies.

This is the tip of the iceberg of what I saw and disclosed in my book.

INTRODUCTION

It is May 12. 2018, two days before my 85th birthday, and my body seems to be slowing down as I move closer to a hundred years of age. Oh well, that is of no significance since I know My Lord and look forward to seeing him face to face in heaven.

Several people have asked me to write a book about my life because I lived overseas for almost twenty-three-years, when I lived overseas, plus another dozen years when my primary home in the USA, on international travel. There was a lot of fun, a lot of frustrations, some perilous times, many lonely and boring days and nights, but for some reason, I was never afraid. I keep asking myself, would anyone really want to read about that?

My family perhaps. But others? After all, some of the story will surely sound fictional.

I often think of the good old clays and bad old days and the current events too. I celebrated my 1st wedding anniversary almost two months ago. I had been married twice before, but they were "destined" to fail: however. I have the three most wonderful children in the world from those marriages. I also brag about my six fantastic grandchildren.

This time, I married a "girl" that I met in 1953 while stationed at Pinecastle AFB Base outside Orlando, FL… She was dating my buddy, and I was dating one of her friends. They were later married after we had all separated to make our marks on the world. He died almost five years just before my surprise 80th birthday party that they had sponsored. Edith and I married last year, a union that will last until one of us is called home to be with The Lord.

Note: Names of people have been changed to protect the innocent.

Statements and descriptions are my personal beliefs and/or opinions.

Dates of some events are not accurate due to elapsed time.

CONTENTS

ABOUT MY STORY iii

INTRODUCTION v

Chapter 1 My Early Years - 1933-1951 1

Chapter 2 in the US Air Force - 1951-1955 12

Chapter 3 Lockheed Employment – 1955-1961 40

Chapter 4 Lockheed Employment - 1961-63 50

Chapter 5 Indonesia - 1962-1963 58

Chapter 6 Pakistan - 1963-1964 70

Chapter 7 Azores Islands, Scotland, Spain & Libya - 1964-1967 82

Chapter 8 LOCKHEED EMPLOYMENT - Iran: 1967-1977 96

Chapter 9 Operating out of England - 1977-1981 130

Chapter 10 Lockheed Employment - 1981-1990 146

Chapter 11 Marketing & Conclusions - 1990-2025 ... 168

Addendum: End Times 187

Photos 190

Chapter 1
My Early Years - 1933-1951

My birth took place on May 14, 1933, in a less-than-humble shack in Irwin County, GA. The officials even got that wrong when they recorded it as August 17, so that was not an auspicious beginning. My parents eventually had it corrected. I had thirteen brothers and sisters. My father had been married before; his wife had seven children before she died. My mother was also previously married, had four children (one died as a baby), and her husband was killed. Afterward, my parents married, and the last three of us were born. I was the baby.

We were sharecropping farmers until much later, when we bought a farm. The first thought I remember about farming was, "There's got to be a better way to make a living." My mother was the hardest-working woman I have ever seen, much like my wife, Edith. She worked all the time and kept singing gospel songs. My father must have raised kids to keep from working—and almost succeeded. Then the children started leaving home, and finally it was just him and me to help my mother, which meant she carried most of the load. If she ever complained, it was only to the Lord. She was forever thankful that we were on a farm so that we could have food to eat during those years of the Great Depression. We moved a lot, trying to make a living, so I cannot recall all the places and dates.

Bill Walls | Memoirs

We lived in Moultrie, GA, for a while, then Okeechobee, FL, and later Rebecca, GA, where I started school in 1939. I looked forward to starting, but the first day was enough. I never told this to anyone but remembered those feelings when my daughter started school in Cambridge, England, in 1977. She was so eager to begin, but the next morning, when I told her it was time to go to school, she informed me that she had already been to school and did not need to go back.

My eldest brother, Dover, had "migrated" to Hogansville, GA, in the 1920s, where he found a good job and purchased a farm near LaGrange. He was living in Hogansville, and I don't know what transpired, but he wanted to tend the farm. At that time, it was just my mother and father, my two youngest brothers, Milford and Luther, and me. That was my next home, probably beginning around early 1940. The earth was red clay, and I don't believe many things would grow in it. I went to Hillcrest School while we unsuccessfully tried to exist. I'm uncertain, but I believe we moved into LaGrange that fall, where my mother, Milford, and Luther found jobs.

On December 7, 1941, the Japanese bombed Pearl Harbor in Hawaii, bringing the USA into World War II. My parents were distraught, knowing that their sons and others would be put in harm's way, and that the USA would suffer in many ways.

My brother Dewitt had joined the Army Combat Engineers around 1936. Herman was the first to be drafted, followed by Milford in 1944, and finally Luther in 1945. All the others were either too old or I was too young. Dewitt was critically wounded by a bomb and spent many months in hospitals; Herman suffered from distress due to his involvement in battles in Europe; Milford, at the age of nineteen, was killed by a Japanese mortar in the Philippines; and Luther's eardrums were severely damaged during basic training. He became totally deaf without specially made hearing aids.

In the meantime, we moved back to South Georgia in early 1942 to tend one of the farms owned by a wealthy cousin. This was one of the best places we had lived so far. We still had Milford and Luther at home; they were hard workers, and before long, our father pulled them out of school to work on the farm, as he had done with all the children previously. I believe all of them had to stop school prior to the seventh grade, some as early as the fourth grade, because he felt no one needed more education than that. My mother never contradicted him on any decision, as she felt the man was the head of the house. She was about four feet eleven inches and never weighed a hundred pounds, but she stood tall and told him, "That is never going to happen to me," as she wanted at least one of her children to receive an education. He knew the subject was closed.

I went to Waterloo School through the seventh grade. (Waterloo is less than seven miles from Irwinville, the area of my birth.) It must have been over a mile from our house at that time to the school in Waterloo, and we had to walk it—not bad except in the winter.

Sidney Hester, who would become my closest neighbor and friend, was the first kid to greet me at school. After a few minutes, he said, "Where are you from, boy?" I said, "North Georgia," and he said, "I thought you sounded like a Yankee!" I still can't believe it!

The next year, we moved to another of my cousin's farms. This one was about halfway to my school and located close to a nice fishpond. One day, when there was an infrequent lull in work, Luther and I took our cane polls and went fishing. We were not getting any bites from fish, just bites from mosquitoes, horseflies, and various insects, so we decided to stick the ends of our poles in the bank and go for a walk. When we returned, his pole was missing; then we spied it about thirty feet away, moving toward the middle of the pond. He said, "That's a big fish; I'm going to get it." He jumped in, quickly swam out, grabbed the pole, and started swimming back, shouting, "It's really a big one." About that time, the big "fish" surfaced, and I shouted, "Luther, you have a gator!" After taking a quick glance, he let go of the pole and set a speed record back to shore. We surmised that a fish got the bait and the alligator got the fish. I made a mental note that this might not be a preferred swimming hole.

Note: Too bad I speak Yankee, as this would sound better in a "South Georgian" accent.

    This is where I got my first paid job. When we caught up on our work, my family took any job available to help buy food. My cousin asked Milford and Luther to hoe a field of cotton at fifty cents a day each and reluctantly paid me twenty-five cents—from daylight to dark. It's a miracle that I didn't demolish the cotton and leave the grass and weeds. I hated picking cotton more than any other job. I certainly didn't want to lose the lucrative job, though.

Time kept ticking by, and 1944 arrived. Then Milford was drafted and went off to war. My mother had already received notification about Dewitt's severe injuries, but she could do nothing but pray for her children.

Our finances were beginning to improve slightly. I already had an old bicycle; Luther had an old car, and my father bought an old Model T Ford. We were able to see an occasional movie in town. Rationing of several items—including gasoline, kerosene, flour, sugar, and more—began at the start of the war and continued until after it ended, so we were limited in what we could buy. You had to use ration book coupons to purchase many things! Candy, Cokes, and many snack foods were hard to find because of that. My family had no idea when the Great Depression ended; for us, it became a little more bearable in the mid-1940s, but the war continued, our troops were still being killed and maimed, so there was little reason to rejoice at our extra pocket change. We could only continue working.

The fateful day came in 1945: we received notice that Milford had been killed in action! How can a family get over this? With great difficulty. It was not made easier when Luther was drafted. But life went on somehow. The end of the war created mixed emotions for me; although I was happy that our troops would be coming home, I was sad that I didn't have an opportunity to go to war, as I felt I had a debt to pay to someone! It was several years before I quelled those emotions.

In 1946, I graduated from the seventh grade at Waterloo and began the eighth grade at Irwin Ville—my place of birth—that fall. High school was grades eight through eleven then; the twelfth grade was added beginning in 1951, so I was in the "Lucky Class," which would graduate in 1950.

My mother had been quietly saving every penny she could and had accumulated a few hundred dollars. She discovered that a nearby farm was for sale, then went to the bank and used that as a down payment on the farm. Fortunately, she had put it in her name; otherwise, we would not have been landowners for very long. Finally, we had a home!

The Lord had really blessed us, although I did not know Him at the time. We had electricity; I didn't need a kerosene lamp anymore to study at night. We continued to work on the farm and take other jobs as available, and soon we enclosed the back porch, bought an electric pump for the well, built an indoor bathroom (which seemed indecent but was convenient), and made several other improvements. Life became almost comfortable.

Luther returned from the army, got married, and moved to Jacksonville, FL, to work. He left his old car and told me he would give me half of anything I could get for it. One Sunday, while my parents were taking an afternoon nap, I took one of my friends for a ride in it because I had been driving for quite a while (I was already thirteen). We made it almost a mile down the unpaved country road before a Highway Patrol car with two officers pulled up behind us. My buddy spotted it and started staring out the back window while pointing back. Of course, this indicated something was going on, so their siren caused me to pull over. One of the officers was nosy enough to ask for my driver's license, and I confessed that I didn't have one. His next question was, "How old are you?" For some reason, I said I was fifteen. He told me I must get a license as soon as I was sixteen, and that he better not catch me driving without one again. He wanted

My Early Years – 1933-1951

to know whether my father knew I had the car, and I told him that he was taking a nap. He told me to get in the passenger's seat and said he would drive me home and wake my father. His partner would follow in the patrol car. Something about the situation alarmed me, especially his decision to drive. I kept quiet, though. He started the engine and began screaming, "The brakes don't work! How do you stop it?" I said, "It's easier going uphill, but you can tear it down otherwise, and if that doesn't stop the car in time, run it into the ditch." I could see he was a slow learner. My father confirmed he was not aware I was driving around and graciously accepted the "ticket." The officer said, "I told your son he better get a driver's license." He failed to say, "after he is sixteen."

On my 14th birthday, my parents went with me to the Highway Patrol station in their Model T Ford. They found seats while I went to an officer and proudly announced that I was there to get my license, confirming that it was my sixteenth birthday. The licensing officer laughed at my eagerness. While I was taking the written exam, my arresting officer came in and said, "I know this boy. He can drive because I gave him a ticket for driving without a license and told him to get one." He patted me on the back for following his advice. After completing the written exam, I was told to get into the car and drive around the block. I don't believe he wanted to ride in the old car. Of course, its brakes didn't work either; however, that was no problem. Reverse gear was engaged by pushing a pedal between the brake and clutch, and a passenger would never know how you stopped so quickly. As soon as I walked back into the patrol station, I received my license and was wished "Good traveling." I did all the family driving after that, which made each of us happy in his or her own way. Best of all, I started driving us to Waterloo Baptist Church almost every Sunday. The only thing I knew about this was that it made my mother very happy.

Concurrently with all of this, I was attending high school and playing basketball. We did not have a school football or baseball team, but we did have a great basketball team. At one point, we had a seventy-eight-game winning streak, including two state championships. Our team outscored the opposition by an average of two to one during the regular season, and even our water boy played in a few games. I was not the star, although no one enjoyed it more than I did. Irwin Ville was proud of the team, and we had a full house at home games. Many people even attended away games. In 1951, a year after I graduated, our school closed, and everyone had to go to Ocilla for high school. It was a long time coming, but the town instituted a Basketball Hall of Fame around 1993 and inducted all of us into it. There was a parade and the usual fanfare. I was not able to attend, so they sent me gifts.

From age eight upwards, I had "crushes" on special girls throughout the years, but none were included in plans as I had no real goals then.

I discovered my poetic talents in high school when one of my teachers assigned each of us to write a poem, which we would have to stand before the class and read. I moaned and groaned, telling everyone, including myself, that there was no way I could do it. The night before the "fatal" day, it all came to me, so I grabbed a pen and paper. The words flowed

My Early Years – 1933-1951

out and filled an entire page. I was elated with my handiwork. The next morning, when it came my turn to read, I proudly stood before the class and began:

"Springtime, springtime. Springtime, springtime, springtime, springtime, springtime,"

Continuing until I had read the entire page. By then, the entire class was roaring with laughter, almost drowning out the choking and gasping noises made by our teacher. Just before strolling back to my seat, I hesitated and waited for the laughter to subside, then said,

"By the way, the name of my poem is 'springtime.'"

I proudly returned to my seat amid the cheers and laughter, although realizing that the teacher would probably find a way to strangle me if she ever recovered. When she was finally able to speak, she gave me a good grade for "intestinal fortitude," without mentioning a possible career as a poet.

I finished high school the week of my 17th birthday. A basketball scholarship was not possible because I was not tall enough, even though I played on a championship team in high school. Baseball was out of the question because I was a lousy pitcher and didn't want to run around in the hot sun chasing the ball at any other position (I couldn't catch it anyway). I didn't have any money for college either and was sure that they had little to tell me that was important.

I thought it might be worthwhile trying for a sports scholarship. I didn't want to go north because it's too cold, so I tried the Gators first. I was not tall enough for baseball and not good at it. The football coach asked me what position

I wanted to play, and I said, "Football." He didn't understand and repeated the question, and I repeated my answer. After the third go-around, I realized why he was a coach: he was not the brightest light in the room. I carefully explained that they could wrap me in pigskin and the muscular quarterback could sail me over everyone toward the end zone. If I came up a little short, I would just trot across the line and lie down on the turf for a touchdown. We would never lose a game. The coach was so ecstatic that he wrapped his big hands around my throat, then told the squad that I was so good that I should also have an opportunity to be the star speed swimmer. I was cheered as I was given a large escort to the Gator pool and thrown into the pool, which was a pond on the edge of the swamp. I quickly learned that there were powerful swimmers in the pond, and I set a new swim and escape record. It appeared that outstanding sportsmen lived dangerous lives: war was less risky. (This was a step away from my truthful story to show why I would never attempt comedy. I could earn more by farming, but I served God and received enormous riches in Heaven.)

I deeply regretted it, but I broke my mother's heart; I moved to Jacksonville, FL, and worked as a driver for a grocery store, earning a "whopping twenty-five dollars a week (before taxes)." I lived with my widowed sister and her two sons. It was difficult for the two of us to earn enough to buy food and pay the bills, so I could never prosper. I loved them, though, so it was worthwhile, although I often thought about how good it had been back on the farm in comparison.

Luther and his wife lived nearby. He had been to an automobile mechanic school on the GI Bill, so he had a good job, although he was suffering from inner ear problems caused by injuries he sustained during his army service. He would have several inner ear operations in the coming years and finally be forced to quit work. He spent a lot of time trying to reduce the pain and made custom hearing aids in attempts to prolong his hearing capabilities.

Jobs were scarce, but I was interviewed for one that might have been better. The manager of a large company talked with me about the job and asked about my experience. When I told him I had none, he said they only hired people with experience. I replied, "How does anyone get experience if no one hires anyone without experience?" He thought for several seconds and said I had a good question.

Chapter 2
in the US Air Force - 1951-1955

I joined the USAF when I was eighteen, certain that I could teach the officials a few things, forgetting that my training thus far had been as a serf. A large group of us from North Florida and South Georgia boarded a troop train and departed Jacksonville on June 26, 1951, for Lackland AFB, San Antonio, TX. This was during the Korean War, so most had joined the Air Force to avoid being drafted into the Army, whereas I wanted to join. I had four brothers, two nephews, and two brothers-in-law who served during WWII. One brother and one nephew were killed when they were nineteen years old; the other three brothers and both brothers-in-law were wounded, most severely, so I felt it was up to me to carry on.

After a long, tiresome trip, we were awakened in the wee hours of the morning by a group outside the train shouting bad things at someone. It occurred to me that perhaps I should shout back and tell them they woke us, but I suddenly realized they were talking to me too—they were "asking" us to disembark. After we stumbled off the train, they impolitely advised us that they were drill instructors and would make us sorry we had left home. I wished I was back on the farm trying to keep pace with Mama! Those nasty men were right. At least I was among a large group of Southerners who spoke the same language since we came from the same general area.

About seventy of us were housed in a two-story barracks. At about four the next morning, we were awakened by our drill instructor shouting, "Fall out!" Everyone hastened outside, promptly getting into the same columns we had been taught the previous day, but he was not happy with our speed. He told us to fall back into the barracks to do it all over again. I decided to impress him with a little speed and zipped past everyone in the dark until my feet became entangled with another pair, and I skidded on my knees. The instructor was not favorably impressed with my footwork.

My hobbling suddenly caused concern, so I was told to walk about twenty miles—or so it seemed (about a quarter of a mile)—for sick call. I told the doctor I wanted to return to the barracks where all my friends were, but he decided there was no suitable place on base; therefore, I would be put in a hospital ward where they could give me therapy. It seemed I had cracked some essential item in my right knee. Every day, I was put in a wheelchair and wheeled to the therapy area and told to call the ward when the doctor finished so someone could wheel me back. I didn't think the "wheeler" enjoyed the job, so I pushed the chair back to the ward every time.

Thirty days later, the doctor decided they couldn't do anything further (I think he was referring to my attitude) and that I would be returned to duty. As a parting shot, I told the doctor I wanted to return to my old barracks and friends (I'd known them for a whole day).

In The US Air Force – 1951-1955

The officer in charge of our squadron almost listened to my wishes before telling me where my next unit was housed. I was sure he had worked everything out for me, so I strolled over and found about seventy Yankees from New York and New Jersey lurking in the barracks. They called me "Johnny Reb," and I called them Yankees until we finished basic training in September. I feel that I furthered their education, and we even became friends. I received my first stripe, promoted from Basic Airman to Airman 1st Class.

In September, a group of USAF officials from Colorado Springs came to Lackland AFB to recruit tough outdoorsmen from among those finishing basic training. One of my Yankee friends heard about it and rushed to tell me. Since I felt tough at that time and had been outside when my parents made me work, that seemed to be the kind of job I was suited for. There were reportedly more than thirty thousand men undergoing basic training, so we knew we had to rush to sign up before the quota was filled. On the day of the briefing, there were fewer than twenty volunteers in the room, so we smiled at our fortune. A few resigned after hearing about our "opportunity" to spend a lot of time hiking across the Great Divide mountains in the middle of winter to learn arctic survival, mountain climbing, and other dangerous skills. We would live off the land (try to kill or trap enough game to eat), learn how to escape from behind enemy lines, and all kinds of exciting things. The day we boarded the old C-47 aircraft to fly to Colorado, there were only seventeen recruits; certainly not a big percentage of the airmen at Lackland were tough outdoorsmen.

We arrived well after midnight to find everything covered with snow and our barracks without heat. There was no mattress or bedding on any bed. We wore our summer uniforms because it had been extremely hot at Lackland. I wanted to be back on the farm with my parents. I would have done all the work and let them rest. A couple of hours later, our bedding was delivered, but there was still no heat.

Our unit was on a corner of Camp Carson, Colorado—an Army Ranger and mule packer camp. Now those are tough outdoorsmen!

The next morning was invigorating, and the sights were fantastic. The camp was at the foot of Cheyenne Mountain with Pikes Peak in the background, and a layer of snow covered everything. Even though I was still cold, I knew this was life for me. Now it became understandable why I left the farm. Something in the back of my mind kept bugging me, though; it seemed too good to be true.

Officials spent a few hours briefing us about the training program. We already knew they required arctic survival instructors, who would be responsible for teaching flight crews from the Air Force, Army, Navy, and Marines how to survive in arctic conditions if they were shot down or made an emergency landing in such areas. We would teach part of that in classrooms and then take them on a trip in the mountains for the rest of their education. The current briefing expanded on this.

In addition to arctic survival training, there was a need for pararescuemen, but there was no discussion of that because we were now preparing for a one-month stay in the Rocky

In The US Air Force – 1951-1955

Mountains near Denver to begin training in earnest. This would entail a 130-mile hike back and forth across the mountains to learn all the skills we would eventually teach. (It seemed more sensible to watch a movie and look at pictures, plus a little classroom instruction.)

We were to purchase enough food for the first twelve days because we would live off the land during that time, after which a plane would airdrop dehydrated food for the remainder of the trip. Each of us was allowed to carry a gun—just in case we ran into some BIG game that wanted to eat us while we were hunting smaller game to survive. There was much more, but we were finally prepared for the big day.

We climbed onto trucks for the ride to our starting point somewhere south of Denver. Snow had continued to accumulate, a prelude to things to come. Upon arrival, everyone offloaded and headed up a mountain slope, halting at a place that could be called "almost level," though the ground was covered in snow. The seventeen students were divided into pairs for the entire trip. There were four instructors, one of whom was a civilian. My partner was an Indian named Red Hale, who had spent his entire life on a reservation, so it was doubtful that a South Georgia boy was going to teach him much about survival. My backpack contained food for the twelve days (which I desperately hoped would be enough, but fearfully doubted); a mess kit for cooking (although I had no idea how to use it); a double arctic sleeping bag; parachute silk (to make a teepee whenever possible, as this was much preferred to a tent); extra clothing; fishing tackle; a magnetic compass; and much more. It was very heavy.

We continued heading upward as we practiced celestial navigation, using the sun, moon, planets, and stars to find our way. We also used the unreliable magnetic compasses, which point somewhat toward magnetic north. Each person took turns using both methods of navigation. Several other skills were being taught simultaneously. The snow was getting deeper, and the temperature was dropping.

Note: This was the fall of 1951; therefore, exact dates, times, and the sequence of some events cannot be recalled.

We were a few thousand feet above sea level and above the timberline for part of the journey, with temperatures around -30°F. Then we ran into a blizzard during a night hike. There was no shelter, so we could only "hunker down" for the rest of the night. I climbed into my double arctic sleeping bag with my arctic parka and boots on and finally got warm. I failed to mention earlier that we had a yodeler in the group who, as he did every morning, woke me with his detested yodel. To make matters worse, he was shaving while wearing slacks and a light sweater, while I was struggling to wear my sleeping bags.

We arrived at Arapaho Pass, which had disappeared from my perspective—simply a bird's-eye view of nothing but air for a long stretch. The instructors advised that this was where we would learn how to belay across a void in a path. The middle of the rope is secured to the person being belayed, while someone on one end—or, if possible, on both ends—wraps the rope around their body in a special way to prevent it from moving too fast. The person hoping to survive the trip tries to find a place to plant their feet to "walk" across the void. Rope is played out on one end and taken in on the other to ensure the "victim" does not fall "forever" if they step off into the void. It can be done to get the first person around the void to set up the ideal belay, but the yodeler took an end of the long rope and pranced around as if there were a paved sidewalk on the Pass. I'm still not sure what he was stepping on. Everyone made it around without incident, although I wished for a bottle of oxygen to restore my breath. We would often use a form of belaying for rock climbing and rappelling (jumping backwards down the sheer face of a cliff).

Sometime later, three men were injured in a relatively small avalanche and had to be evacuated on makeshift stretchers to the nearest road. I never saw them again, so they must have found a more adventurous job.

Most of us ran short of food before the end of the first twelve days; therefore, we started trying to catch or kill enough food to survive. Red Hale and I killed a porcupine, but I told him to keep my half. He cooked it over an open fire and stored most of it in his backpack. The next day, I was starving and gladly accepted a piece of the porcupine. It was better than any chicken or steak I had ever tasted. I put my last tidbit of bread on the trigger of a bird trap I made. I believe the bird sat on the trigger while eating the bread. Naturally, the trap never worked.

We were headed down into a valley where it was much warmer when two forest rangers drove up and offered us a deer they had taken from a poacher. I am sure this was a planned way to keep us from starving or losing face; however, we didn't question it. We made a rock oven by digging a large hole in the ground, putting several large rocks in it, and then building a fire inside the area. When the rocks were very hot, we covered the embers and wrapped the deer with parachute silk (someone else had skinned and cleaned the deer). Then we laid the deer on some of the hot rocks while placing others around and on top of it. We covered all of this with dirt so the heat from the rocks would cook the deer for a few hours. It was fantastic—much better than the cold porcupine that Red Hale had shared with me. Very few of us found any fish or wild game to eat.

The cliff face above a valley was an ideal place to practice rock climbing and rappelling down the face, and we enjoyed it. The goal in all of this was to keep your head from being the primary contact point with the rocks.

Escape and evasion—or vice versa—is a main focus in arctic survival training, especially during wartime. Those of us who were to become instructors needed to teach flight crews how to survive if they bailed out or crash-landed in arctic conditions. If that happened behind enemy lines, they had to know how to evade the enemy and escape. Those who became pararescuemen might have to jump behind enemy lines—North Korea at that time—to provide medical treatment to a flight crew and then use their knowledge to help them evade the enemy and escape. Our training and subsequent teaching employed specially trained crews to act as the enemy while we were in the mountains. The "enemy" was taught how to locate and apprehend us, which was beginning to seem like a cakewalk for them because they could probably see our footprints in the snow from an airliner flying overhead. Evidently, that is why this phase of

In The US Air Force – 1951-1955

our training took place later. I was beginning to feel sorry for anyone I was supposed to train or try to rescue.

Our food airdrop of military "C" rations went as scheduled. The real energy source was Beef Pemmican Bars—not very tasty or filling, but loaded with protein. Somehow, I still stayed hungry.

We finally made it through the mountains to our rendezvous point, thirty days and 130 miles from the start of our trek. The trucks stopped at the first town so we could buy some real food. I purchased two pints of ice cream and about twelve large bars of candy, hoping we would stop again to replenish our supplies. (I had failed to include sweets in my supplies for the one-month tour of the Rocky Mountains.) I finished the ice cream and started on the candy before realizing that my stomach was now used to porcupine and pemmican. The Lord has blessed me with a strong digestive system, which allowed me to retain the sweets and keep smiling—although the smiles were rather weak. It was not necessary for the trucks to make a replenishment stop after all.

Our training program continued, including hours with headsets on, listening to a never-ending series of dits and dots as we learned Morse code. I guessed it was not meant for a South Georgia boy to understand dits and dots or foreign languages either.

In late February 1952, I started analyzing my situation:

If I wanted to be an arctic survival instructor, I would probably spend half my time in the mountains with flight crews, plus time teaching in a classroom. It was doubtful I could teach them to love porcupine meat; how to navigate by looking at the stars, sun, moon, and planets; how to trap and hunt game or fish when they weren't there; and I certainly couldn't communicate in dits, dots, and dashes.

To become a pararescueman, I would need to learn emergency medical treatment, undergo parachute training, and much more. In the end, I might have to jump out of a perfectly good airplane behind enemy lines in Korea (hoping the Koreans would either not see me or assume I was one of them), perform medical treatment on the flight crew, and help them escape. That sounded a bit dangerous.

During the briefings at Lackland AFB in September 1951, it was emphasized that we could leave the program at any time we desired and could go to any school of our choice simply by making our wishes known. I did not want to be a quitter, but I did not see any future in this job.

I made an appointment to see our squadron commander and shuffled down to his office. I started reciting the pitiful excuse I had memorized, but he simply said, "Oh, you want out? I'm sorry to lose you. What school would you like to attend?" I said I would like to attend A&E School (Aircraft and Aircraft Engine Mechanic School). Within a few days, my orders were issued to depart for Sheppard AFB at Wichita Falls, Texas.

After saying goodbye to Red Hale, Willie Williams, and other friends, I was whisked away. Ironically, I met Willie in Spain fourteen years later.

It was probably March 1952 when I arrived in Wichita Falls, meaning I had spent the first summer of my USAF duty in

In The US Air Force – 1951-1955

the hot state of Texas, followed by the winter in Colorado, and then back to Texas for another summer. It seemed I should reverse that trend.

While at Sheppard AFB, I decided I should be a pilot, so I took a series of tests and a flight physical exam to qualify for Aviation Cadet training. Much to my dismay, after all that, there were so many college graduates with the same idea that I never received notice to go to the school.

The A&E school was very interesting. We learned how to repair aircraft and their engines. The problem was that the classroom training and hands-on work were on old B-29 bombers, which were becoming obsolete. This was not of great significance, though, because the school taught basics that would apply to any aircraft.

Most things I recall about my stay at the base were frequent KP (kitchen duty), garbage detail, and other work duties. These had been prevalent at Lackland and Camp Carson and seemed inevitable at future assigned locations. However, there was an obnoxious "person" (not to be named here) at Sheppard who took away the joy of breathing (maybe that's a slight exaggeration). I somehow managed to endure everything.

That fall, as we prepared to graduate from A&E School, a few of us were told that the Air Force had a shortage of aircraft electricians and that we had been selected to proceed to the school at, of all places, Chanute AFB, Rantoul, IL, about 150 miles from Chicago—thus another cold winter, indicating the trend continued (north for winter, south for summer).

The electrical school was exciting and enlightening, especially when a friend would charge a capacitor and toss it to me when the instructor wasn't looking. If I caught it, the electrical shock would "light up my eyes"; if I turned away, it would discharge into another part of my body and still "light up my eyes." I seldom did that to others. Seriously, this is dangerous and should not be done.

One thing I learned outside the classroom is that I never want to live in Chicago! The wind seemed to blow from all directions at the same time, and in winter, it felt colder than during a blizzard above the timberline in the Rocky Mountains. The only praise I have for the city is, "It has a nice museum, and you can escape the vicious wind by going inside—assuming it is open." Rantoul was a small town with nothing of interest to me.

Upon graduation from electrical school in March 1953, I was awarded a stripe for my grades and promoted to Airman Second Class (A2C), but I was still a long way from the rank of general. Everyone waited anxiously to learn where they would be assigned—Korea, another overseas location, or stateside. I was sent to Pinecastle AFB, Orlando, FL.

It was a pleasure to discover that we had new two-story dormitory-style barracks, with two men to a room. My roommate was Joe Newman, a nice, compatible guy. However, we learned that the men living on the first floor below us had an attitude problem. When Joe and I came in at night and quietly removed our shoes, put on our wooden shower clogs, and walked across the hardwood floor, our downstairs neighbors would beat on the ceiling with broom handles. Of course, we responded by tap dancing on the floor

In The US Air Force – 1951-1955

while wearing the wooden shoes. Our neighbors were Alvin Harris and Earl Schlicht. The four of us—all electricians—later became friends.

At that time, Pinecastle was the home base for a wing of jet fighter aircraft and jet trainer aircraft. Joe and I were offered jobs in Reclamation, a type of crash recovery team.

The attractive part of the job was that we would work for twenty-four hours—sleeping in the Reclamation hut, playing games, or doing other work—being available in case a plane crashed on the runway, and then we would be off duty for forty-eight hours. We accepted (though it's possible we were simply told that would be our job). Alvin and Earl were already assigned to the electric shop.

The most interesting—but sad—job we did was to attempt to find and recover one of our fighter aircraft that was reported missing. Reports came in that it had exploded in the air over a lake near Orlando. A master sergeant, a sergeant, and A2C Walls took a Weasel (a small amphibious vehicle) to the lake and launched it. A man among a group of civilians on the bank claimed to have seen the aircraft explode and saw a large piece fall into the water. We saw fuel on top of the water, so the master sergeant told me to take off my fatigue uniform, leaving me in shorts, and jump in to see if I could locate anything in the area. I was reluctant to do that since there was so much fuel, but more so because I didn't want to expose myself in shorts. I jumped instead of diving, and God took care of me—my bare feet hit the broken canopy of the aircraft, cutting both. My head would have been severely damaged if I had elected to dive. The pilot was still strapped in his seat, so I crawled into the cockpit and

24

tried to free him. Being unsuccessful, we went ashore in the Weasel and brought the end of a steel cable attached to a winch on one of our large recovery vehicles. I jumped back (carefully) into the water and attached the cable to the section of aircraft. The truck winched it out, and then the pilot's body was removed.

A few months later, my lifestyle changed; the fighter aircraft departed Pinecastle AFB and were replaced by "elderly" B-47 bombers, part of Strategic Air Command under General Curtis LeMay. Reclamation was disbanded or changed. Joe Newman and I moved to the electric shop to work alongside our downstairs neighbors, Alvin Harris and Earl Schlicht. The base was put on a twelve-hour workday, seven days per week—a big change from Reclamation. It seemed that all existing bases sent their worst aircraft to new bases to meet required numbers because we felt we were experiencing an excessive number of problems.

Strategic Air Command (SAC) kept bombers in the air continually, so we had to provide total maintenance support around the clock.

Most of us met some nice girls. Al dated Edith Harrell, who worked at the local drugstore, and I dated one of her friends. Those were the days when drugstores had soda fountains, and that was where Edith worked until she started keeping the books for the owner. Some of the guys liked to tease Edith by ordering a glass of water, then putting a plastic coaster on top and turning it upside down on the counter. If the glass was lifted, all the water gushed out onto the counter. (This is not recommended these days—you'd probably be arrested.) She quickly learned to put a bucket under the edge

In The US Air Force – 1951-1955

of the counter and slide the glass off over it, thus catching the water. She had an analytical mind at an early age, so the fun was soon eliminated. Killjoy! However, we soon learned that Edith was an excellent cook, making it easier to forget her trick-squashing.

SAC held a bombing competition each year, including our unit, the 321st Bomb Wing. Incidentally, the only medal I was ever awarded was one the Wing had won during WWII. I believe we were supposed to buy one and wear it, but I did not because I felt I had not earned it. They only held the competition once before I was discharged from the Air Force. I was selected to go, indicating that I got stuck! The "stuckees" loaded our toolboxes and clothes on a KC-97 aircraft, which was used to refuel the B-47s in flight, and were flown to Barksdale AFB in Louisiana, where our two bombers were to be staged. The small maintenance team would support them, hopefully. I believe the B-47s would take off from Barksdale and bomb a target in Kansas, hopefully. Even though precision bombsights had not yet been built, B-47s usually did an excellent job, giving me hope that we would hit Kansas—or even an unpopulated area. We managed to keep the planes in good condition for their "any-hour" takeoff time. Their departures were on time, and they always came back without any bombs. They were not supposed to return with bombs, which made me think about Kansas again (or maybe Mississippi or New York). That was silly, though. Oops! At the end of the competition, someone told me we came in last place. I kept waiting for a state to claim they had been bombed and want the USA to declare war. (Just kidding!) The Commander of SAC apparently did not hold me personally responsible.

We returned to Orlando and our twelve-hours-a-day, seven-days-a-week work schedule. This seemed routine compared to the as-needed, twenty-four-hours-a-day schedule during the bombing exercise.

We even found time to teach some of the girls how to water-ski. Ed, one of our friends, had a twelve-foot boat with a 25 HP outboard motor—not ideal for pulling a skier. We used a nylon parachute cord as a tow rope. If you've never done this, don't. It's like a bungee cord. You get ready to be pulled out of the water as the boat races off with its 25 HP engine and the tow rope stretches. Suddenly, you are jerked onto the top of the water—hopefully still wearing skis. Now you are gaining on the boat as the rope tries to retract to its normal length. This creates another problem: when your rope has retracted and goes slack, you try to walk on water because you are sinking. You try all kinds of maneuvers to take up the slack, and suddenly you are yanked forward when the boat finally takes up the slack and starts stretching the rope again. This process continues until everything is quasi-normal. This is drastically compounded if you cannot afford life jackets, and especially if you suddenly discover that the girl on skis is sinking and neglected to tell you she doesn't know how to swim (or maybe you just weren't listening when she said it). The speedboat trudges along toward her while she attempts to drink enough water to bring the level down below her mouth. We did rescue her, and I believe she gave up skiing. (My advice to everyone is to ensure you have life jackets and try to teach people to swim before taking them skiing.)

In The US Air Force – 1951-1955

One day, Ed and I decided to take our girlfriends to Silver Springs in the twelve-foot speedboat, across lakes and up a river—a quite long trip—so we got an early start because we wanted to make the round trip in a day. We probably didn't do much calculating to be sure it was possible, especially if any time was to be spent at the springs. We still didn't own life jackets, and I think I recall that I was the only swimmer. I was a little concerned about the rough water in the first lake; however, God looked after us. We found the exit into the river and made it safely to Silver Springs a few hours later. A time of fun was had, after which we headed downriver toward home. All was going well until about dark at the most remote place on the trip; it became quiet except for the hoard of mosquitoes attempting to eat us. Yep, the engine gave up the ghost! That explained the lack of noise. Ed fought it but finally decided it was not going to restart. It became so dark that it was impossible to see the shore, and we had no oars, so we kept drifting along, peering in all directions for a light in a home. Finally, there was a light. Now, how do we get there? I was more concerned about the wrath of the fathers of our girlfriends than a few alligators, so I slid overboard and towed the boat toward the light, expecting a 'gator to bite my legs at any moment, and thinking maybe I should have stayed aboard because the fathers might show mercy. Thoughts started coming to me: Are some gators behind me or coming up under me? Wonder if Eleanor will remember me as a hero after I'm gone? Perhaps the Air Force will send a medal to my parents; no, most likely I'll be considered a deserter even though I was consumed by a bunch of gators. Suddenly, my feet touched the ground. We had reached the shore. I tied the boat to a small tree that I bumped into while stepping onto terra firma (good, firm soil) and helped Eleanor out of the boat. All of us headed for the light as a door opened, and we were welcomed inside the house. Things were a little confusing after that: all the explanations, telephone calls to get someone—or anyone—to rescue us. The girls got home. Ed and I were delivered to his car, and we retrieved his boat the next day (I think).

I know whoever might be reading this will wonder, "How did they get into so many 'situations' if they were working all the time?" Right now, seventy years later, I don't remember. Probably just the way GIs do things. I seemed to have a knack for it.

Life carried on at the base. Our wing had been instructed to make plans to become mobile—ready to relocate quickly. An in-route maintenance team was selected. Al, Earl, and I were on the team that would fly to a location on the route to our destination. We would be prepared to repair any B-47 that had problems necessitating a landing there before proceeding.

An advance party was picked to proceed directly to the destination and prepare for the arrival of the aircraft. The remainder of the 321st wing personnel would help launch the aircraft and then fly to the destination.

This was about mid-1954, and we were soon advised that we would be deployed to England in November for a ninety-day mission. All the girls in Orlando received the news, quickly causing deep sadness or a sigh of relief—likely the latter. I'm sure all airmen tried to present a mournful look, just thinking

In The US Air Force – 1951-1955

of the rough duty, when we had hoped for an assignment to assist in the war effort in Korea. (?)

The day of anxiety came, and our small group of in-route repairmen climbed aboard a C-124 (aptly nicknamed "Big Shaky"). The aircraft was heavily loaded, and my arms felt heavy too because I had been promoted to Airman 3rd Class, so I now had three stripes on my sleeves.

The aircraft rumbled down the runway and finally became airborne. We would fly along for a few minutes and suddenly the aircraft would shake. I believe this had something to do with the harmonic frequency of the propellers. It would settle down for a few minutes, then shake again. You could time it.

After a few hundred shakes, we landed in Bermuda. We spent the night and saw the island, then left the next day for the Azores, a small group of islands belonging to Portugal, or part of Portugal. Again, a few hundred shakes, and the old C-124 landed at Lajes Air Base on Terceira Island. This would be our in-route station for the next two days while we hoped all of the B-47s passed by safely as they headed for Morocco (called French Morocco at the time).

Everything went well, so we prepared for "shaking" as we fastened our seat belts and aimed for Sidi Slimane, French Morocco.

One of the B-47 aircraft disappeared over the mountains as it was arriving from Orlando and approaching the base at Sidi. We were all very concerned because our aircraft were old and did not have ejection seats. The only way out was for all four crewmen to drop down the entrance, one at a time. (The aircraft only had three crew members, but a seat had been installed for the crew chief—the mechanic.) We were told that the crew had never escaped that way.

Everyone was elated when all four of them came riding in on donkeys a few days later. Arabs brought them out of the mountains in exchange for the crew's flight helmets—or so I was told. I understood that the plane did not have enough fuel to make it over the mountain range. The pilot slowed the aircraft for the crew to drop out the entrance, one at a time, and he then followed. (Later on, all B-47s were equipped with ejection seats, except the crew chief's seat.)

We were there for several days to maintain the B-47s as they flew missions, probably simulated combat missions. Along with the work, we managed to squeeze in some sightseeing. It was rather desolate, hot, and dusty country—not "totally" safe, because it was still a French colony, hence French Morocco, and the Arabs were fighting for independence.

The next leg of our ninety-day trip was to Lakenheath AB, near Newmarket, England, which would be our home base. Newmarket is a relatively small city but known worldwide for its horse races.

England had gone through terrible bombardment by Nazi aircraft and rockets during WWII, but the British were courageous. They "kept a stiff upper lip" and withstood everything without surrendering; however, when we arrived there nine years later, they were still trying to recover. There was a terrible "smog" in the large cities, especially London, caused by numerous years of burning coal for heating most of the year because of the cold, damp weather. The air was so full of smoke it burned your eyes and affected your breathing. All of the inner-city buildings and statues were blackened by coal soot. Therefore, there was a sense of gloom. A large portion of the people would visit the pubs for a pint of ale and chat with friends as often as possible. (When I returned twenty years later, coal was banned for heating, and a vigorous building cleanup ensued, restoring the true colors of buildings and statues.)

Much of Europe's population reportedly resented having so many American servicemen stationed there, even though the USA had turned the tide against the Nazis and their allies by entering the war on the side of Europe. I heard it said, "U.S. GIs are over: over-paid, over-sexed, and over here. Yankee go home!"

Our barracks was a one-story, open bay, meaning you could see everything inside as soon as you walked in the door on either end. The only heat came from a kerosene stove in the middle of the barracks. A truck was supposed to come around periodically (must have been on February 29th) and fill the fifty-five-gallon drum mounted on a rack outside. Not if—but when—the heat went off around one a.m., someone would walk outside and come back in to report that someone had stolen our drum. There must have been about forty barracks like ours and about fifty men in each, so when your drum was stolen, you would send out a search party to find one with fuel and bring it back. There was a lot of movement in the dark as search parties ran to and fro looking for fuel to "requisition." I was the barracks chief, so everything was always above board.

The bathroom that a multitude of people used was across the street. To have a cold shower in the cold bathroom, it was necessary to cross a small, cold, windy street. It is assumed that a search party had requisitioned (aka stolen) the bathroom fuel drum and it was never replaced. We were told that the coal fire to heat the shower water was "stoked" by a civilian, who evidently was also the driver who delivered the kerosene for the barracks' heaters on February 29. I'm not sure whether anyone tried to skip the shower for the duration of our stay. Probably not—otherwise a group of his ex-friends would have given him a GI bath with a stiff bristle brush.

Tobacco products were very expensive, and smokers cherished U.S. cigarettes. We could buy a ten-pack carton of our best cigarettes in the PX for a dollar and trade it for a night in a nice London hotel, if we had been so inclined. Once in "The Big Smokey," there was a lot to see and do, although we were limited due to the low income GIs received at the time. Low- or no-cost events, such as the Changing of the Guard at Buckingham Palace (the residence of the royal family), Big Ben, the Tower of London, and London Bridge were a few favorites.

One day in January 1955, the electric shop sergeant told me that one of the B-47 aircraft would fly a mission to Norway and I would be going as the support electrician. At the appointed time, the small maintenance team boarded a KC-97 Inflight Refuel Aircraft, which flew us to Gardermoen Air Base near Oslo, Norway. Upon arrival of the B-47, all of us were gathered in the officer's club with counterpart Norwegian Air Force personnel for a Norwegian meal and discussions. Their fighter planes had been scrambled to intercept the bomber, and much discussion related to that.

Apparently, the B-47 ran off and left the interceptors behind, surprising all their officials.

This was a "goodwill" tour to Norway, so we spread goodwill for about a week before returning to England. Fortunately, our aircraft did not require any electrical repairs while we were gone.

When I walked into the shop at Lakenheath, all the electricians and our shop chief began asking questions about the trip. I had to tell them how bad it was—worked hard and no time for fun—but I would volunteer to go on other forthcoming tours to Norway just to spare everyone else the suffering. I was deeply hurt that no one believed my story. That was my last hurrah.

One of the men in our barracks was a good artist and painted an emblem on a pillowcase, which everyone declared to be the electric shop motto. (I won't describe it.) They asked me how we could display it, and naturally I decided that we should run it up the flagpole. Some in the barracks believed it would be taken down the next morning when discovered at reveille; however, I told them I would climb the flagpole and tie the rope at the top so it would take a while to get it down. Off we went down the street to the Orderly Room and the flagpole out front. The pole was a small metal pipe, smaller than I thought, and probably twenty-five feet high. Quite a challenge to climb, especially in cold weather, but I had to make believers out of those who doubted I could shinny up it and tie the rope. I was making good progress upward, but something happened that unnerved me—the pole was moving and, just as I reached the top, my feet touched the ground! The pole had bent like a pretzel! While

I was thinking of ways to straighten a metal pipe in the middle of an English winter so that no one would pay any attention the next day, and wondering if this was the spot where the firing squad would assemble to shoot me if I failed, all of my friends disappeared. I think everyone was trying to find vacancies in another barracks.

As we passed by early the next morning en route to the chow hall, a few people had already noticed the flagpole that had evidently been hit by a freak wind and blown over. I was told late that afternoon that the first sergeant had someone remove the pole and take it to the metal shop for repair. It is very difficult to straighten a metal pipe, so the pole never looked quite the same again. Every time I was tempted to point this out to the first sergeant, I was reminded that some people don't take critique very well. I reluctantly kept quiet.

With all our hard work, time flew by, and suddenly it was March 1955 and time for our return to Florida. Al, Earl, and I boarded the Big Shaky C-124, along with the rest of the in-route maintenance team, and were flown to Lajes Air Base in the Azores. We were there a few days until all our aircraft had arrived in Florida, then we shook all the way home.

A short time after we arrived, I went to Jacksonville, where I saw the most beautiful car of my life sitting in the Chevrolet dealer's showroom. It was bright red and ivory on the outside and inside, with leather seats and a V-8 engine: the hot car of the year, a 1955 Bel Air sports coupe. A car meant for every twenty-one-year-old without much money. Brand new in the showroom window, at a whopping price of $2,450. So I counted my change and gave it to the dealer. I was outta there in a flash.

In The US Air Force – 1951-1955

It didn't take long to get it registered at Pinecastle AFB, and then I began showing it to all my friends. I'm not sure how I told them I was going to pay for it, but it certainly did not include re-enlisting in the Air Force. Of course, Al and I showed it to Edith and all the girls. I don't remember who my girlfriend was at the time, but the whole gang went to Daytona Beach as usual.

Time moved forward as we worked and played, and I kept thinking of my discharge, which was coming up on June 26th of that year, 1955. While pondering my good fortunes, another unwanted experience was waiting to happen.

Another friend and I were enjoying a day off, riding around and flashing my new car while Al, Earl, and everyone else were working. I suggested we drive down to the parking lot at the flight line and pick them up when they got off work to keep them from having to ride the shuttle bus. We were in the parking lot when I spied them, so I started up and drove onto the cement apron to make it easy for them to get into the car. Suddenly, Air Policemen came zipping up and surrounded my car. I didn't think there were that many south of the Mason-Dixon line (a surveyed line running east to west, basically just north of Maryland). I guess they couldn't decide which of them had the honor of shooting me, so I was taken to the office for "waterboarding." When they heard I had not been initiated yet, they settled for questioning. I immediately stated that everything was my fault and my friends should be released, which they soon were. My squadron commander, or first sergeant, or another official finally confirmed that I was not an enemy agent, so I was free to go. It was decided that I would be restricted to the base and my car was kicked off the base for thirty days as punishment. I asked Edith to take it home and use it for a month.

Unfortunately, a couple of weeks later, one of my friends asked if I would like to go to Daytona Beach that Saturday, and I said, "Yes." He reminded me that I was not supposed to leave the base, but that was two weeks ago. The guards did not check cars leaving the base but did a thorough inspection of everyone entering it, so we sailed through, and he dropped me at Edith's house to "borrow" my car. Of course, there were the usual questions: "Are you crazy? How did you get off the base? Why? Are you crazy? How do you think you can get back on the base?" The answers were obvious: Yes. Rode through the gate. I'm not sure. Yes. I have no idea right now, but I have several hours to think about it, and there must be some way. I'll bring the car back to you.

Of course, I got a bad sunburn and still had not solved my problem. It did not seem practical to speed through the base gate and hope no one would see me. I considered climbing a perimeter fence a long way from the gate, but I probably would be eaten by the guard dogs. I wondered whether one of my "buddies" would drive out and let me ride back in the trunk of his car; however, the guards open trunks and even look under cars entering the base. I would consider something else, but what?

I drove to Edith's house and handed the keys to her. Her younger sister, Juanita, walked quietly into the room and said, "Hi Bill, nice car. They are having a dress-up at school tomorrow. Would you let me drive your car?" I was shocked.

I had never heard her say that much. She was normally very quiet, just "hello" or something like that, and my mind was occupied with another problem, so I simply replied, "Sure." She dropped her voice and spoke a few words, which I interpreted as "thank you," so I replied, "No problem." I turned to Edith and suggested that I get in the car trunk, and she could drive through the gate. My reasoning was that a cute little redhead driving a hot car like that would get all the guards' attention. She said, "Sure," and away we went. As expected, she was stopped and the guard asked where she planned to go. Edith told him that she needed to go to the 321st Maintenance Squadron area. Just like that, I was headed for the barracks. Oops! The car stopped suddenly and, seconds later, the trunk lid popped open. My first thought was that the guards were toying with us, and now I'm in big trouble, but worst of all, I had involved her. Never mind, it was Edith yelling that she had been calling me and feared I had suffocated since I didn't answer. She dropped me at the barracks and headed back home.

The next morning, the first sergeant asked what I had done to get the sunburn, and I told him I had laid on the beach at Daytona too long. He said, "Sure you did! You are on restrictions, so you just laid outside the barracks and got burned." He never believed me.

As soon as my month of restriction ended, I went into town to get my car from Edith, and Juanita drifted into the room. In her quiet voice, she said, "Thank you for letting me drive your car. I didn't think you would let me have it because I don't have a driver's license."

"What do you mean?" I asked.

She said, "I told you," and you said, "No problem."

I then learned that the school day she drove was one when each student had to dress like a small girl or boy, as appropriate. I could just imagine her dressed like a seven-year-old girl and driving without a license.

I was told that the soonest I could pick up my discharge was one minute after midnight on June 25 (the morning of the 26th). So I arrived early to be sure I had the right office. When it was handed to me, I could imagine that all the 321st Maintenance Squadron locks were being changed just in case I changed my mind. But I was streaking up the highway to see my parents on the farm.

Chapter 3
Lockheed Employment – 1955-1961

My plan was to spend a few days with my parents, then drive to Marietta, Georgia, to apply for a job with Lockheed Georgia Company, followed by a trip to St. Louis, Missouri, to apply at McDonnell Douglas, and finally to Wichita, Kansas, to seek employment with Boeing or some airline manufacturing company. If I failed to find a good-paying job before September, my Air Force "mustering out" funds would be depleted.

My parents were elated to see me and desperately hoped I would stay home for good. I had visited home a few times while in the Air Force, but now that I was without a job, they hoped I would remain. They were disappointed when I outlined my plans, fearing I would go far away.

I spent about three days taking them shopping and visiting relatives and friends, then left early on June 30th for Marietta. The best route was via U.S. Highway 41, a two-lane road all the way through Atlanta. I arrived at the front gate of Lockheed Georgia and told the guards I was there to apply for a job. They informed me I had to go to the employment office in downtown Atlanta to take an exam. I glanced at the directions and nearly turned north on Highway 41 toward St. Louis, but reluctantly drove back to Atlanta.

At the employment office, I took a lengthy exam followed by an interview. My score was very good, and I apparently didn't look too sloppy. Lockheed urgently needed aircraft electricians, especially those with B-47 experience. They asked how soon I could start. I said, "August 1st," but my interviewer said, "We need you ASAP. How about next Tuesday, July 5th?" Monday was a holiday, so I regretfully agreed and headed back down Highway 41 to the farm. Quite an eventful day!

My mother was ecstatic that I would be working close to home in Georgia and earning much better pay than the twenty-five cents a day I made at my first job ten years earlier. My father almost smiled, which was a sign of happiness.

A few years later, I discovered my father had boasted about my job at Lockheed. It wasn't much to brag about, but I felt fortunate.

I returned to Marietta on Monday, July 4, and rented a room with a shared bathroom at a "rooming house." Marietta was a small town, not yet heavily influenced by Atlanta, which had a population of around 250,000. By 2018, metropolitan Atlanta would likely have close to five million people, impacting Marietta and the entire region within fifty miles.

Tuesday, July 5, 1955, marked the beginning of my career with Lockheed—a company I came to love as much as one can love an organization.

The main building, numbered B-1, where aircraft were built, covered thirty-seven acres under one roof. It had no windows but was fully lit and air-conditioned. There were two stories of engineering, planning, and technical offices on one side, with numerous workshops. The aircraft production lines were in the center and on the opposite side. The most amazing feature was the main floor, made mostly of 2" x 4"

Lockheed Employment – 1961-1963

wood pieces, about eighteen inches long, stood on end. This large building must have contained hundreds of thousands of these pieces. The facility was erected early in World War II for Bell Bomber Company to build B-29 aircraft. Due to a cement shortage, wooden 2x4s were used instead, or so I was told.

A full basement beneath had streets and avenues with vehicular traffic and pedestrians, complete with stop signs but no traffic lights. Numerous offices, a cafeteria, and emergency medical facilities were located there. Several other large buildings, numbered B-2, B-3, etc., were dwarfed by B-1.

Bell closed at the end of the war, and Lockheed reopened the facility around 1950. The U.S. Air Force owned everything and leased it to Lockheed, so many Air Force personnel were on site.

Lockheed-Georgia Company, with about thirty-five thousand employees at its peak, was part of Lockheed Corporation, which had over 130,000 employees worldwide. Some Georgia employees worked outside Marietta in other roles.

When I arrived, Lockheed was manufacturing B-47 aircraft under contract from Boeing, the prime manufacturer. They also had contracts for major repair and overhaul of B-47s. The Lockheed C-130 aircraft program was underway, but no deliveries had been made yet. The C-130 production would become the longest-running cargo aircraft program in history, lasting more than seventy years and continuing into 2025.

My starting job was on the flight line as an aircraft electrician, maintaining new B-47s undergoing flight tests before delivery to the U.S. Air Force. The flight line was about two miles from the B-1 building, across the runways. Operations ran three shifts, Monday to Friday: Day Shift from 7:00 a.m. to 3:45 p.m.; Swing Shift from 3:45 p.m. to 12:30 a.m.; and Graveyard Shift from 12:30 a.m. to 7:00 a.m. I was assigned to the Swing Shift, which paid an eight-cent-per-hour shift bonus. Whoopee! There was plenty of overtime work as well.

The job was easy, working on new aircraft instead of older B-47s like those in Orlando. With my experience, troubleshooting was straightforward.

I occasionally drove to Pine castle Air Force Base to visit friends still in the Air Force, leaving after work on Friday nights (actually 12:30 a.m. Saturday) and returning Sunday night to be at work Monday afternoon. I didn't make many trips before Al received his discharge.

I spoke with my boss about a job for Al just before he got out. He asked if Al could handle the B-47 electrical work like I did. I said, "Probably better." So, he called the employment office and instructed them to give Al the written exam and hire him if he passed. A few days later, we were back together. We worked seven days a week and overtime at night for two or three weeks, then layoffs began. Al was one of the first to go, as layoffs were based on seniority.

I don't remember exactly when, but I got married sometime early in 1956. I was blessed with a wonderful son, Ricky, born February 23, 1957. Shortly after that joyous event, it

Lockheed Employment – 1961-1963

was decided that a divorce should take place before the ink on the marriage license faded.

Meanwhile, I had started college in Atlanta at what would become Georgia State University, attending classes during the day and working on the flight line at night. Later, a University of Georgia center opened in Marietta, so I transferred there and completed another two years.

I majored in law for over two years before switching to physics, which caused me to lose forty-eight quarter hours of good grades since those courses weren't part of the physics curriculum. (One year equals forty-five quarter hours.) After more than two years in Marietta, I attended Oglethorpe University in Atlanta for about two quarters before returning to Georgia State University, where I had started. I had to drive into Atlanta early for my first class and sometimes left the physics lab early to be at Lockheed in Marietta before 3:45 p.m., fortunately, the late lab time applied consistently.

Concurrently, I bowled in two leagues that started at 1:00 a.m. after work.

At some point, I started attending a Holiness church and finally accepted Jesus Christ as my Savior and Lord. Sundays became my day with Ricky. That made life worth living because the rest of the week was so busy that I could only spend short periods with him. Sundays were our special time, starting with church. We didn't have much money, but I was determined to succeed someday if the Lord willed it, and I thank Him for making it possible. One day, all the hard work would pay off.

Late in 1956, my boss told me about a job opening in Engineering Flight Test, so I moved off the flight line to a hangar near the large B-1 building. My supervisor was a very nice and knowledgeable man, Jed Riding.

I was assigned to a special project on a B-47 aircraft. It was classified "top secret" at the time, so I probably shouldn't discuss it now, although 21st-century technology has surpassed what we did.

After completing the B-47 project, I worked on installing skis on a C-130. This was very complicated due to the aircraft's size and the design of the nose landing gear, but we finally retrofitted them. Later, several more sets were installed on U.S. Navy C-130s, enabling support for "Operation Deep Freeze" at the South Pole.

Jed advised me he was transferring to the Field Service Department, where he would travel to advice customers who purchased C-130 aircraft, and asked if I was interested in joining. I decided not to pursue it at the time because I wanted to continue college.

I was still an hourly worker, and I assume the union learned that someone with low seniority was working in Engineering Flight Test because, around mid-1957, I was informed that a person with higher seniority was "bumping" me back to the flight line.

Layoffs continued slowly, making my termination imminent and ending my hopes of a long career with Lockheed. Several men approached me about the upcoming labor union elections and encouraged me to run for Senior Chairman of the flight line swing shift.

Lockheed Employment – 1961-1963

This position would grant me top seniority, making me the last electrician laid off—in essence, the last person on the flight line to lose his job. I was surprised because I wasn't an avid union man and had no idea what the role entailed. Most of all, I thought it unfair that more senior employees might lose their jobs while I kept working. After voicing my concerns, most electricians assured me they were willing to sacrifice their jobs if necessary. I won the election by a landslide and was unopposed every year thereafter, so I did the job to the best of my ability.

When the first C-130s were built between 1953 and 1956, electrically controlled propellers were installed, but problems delayed delivery. Lockheed retrofitted all aircraft with 3-bladed, hydraulically controlled propellers from another company and continued installing them for several years. These were the "A" model or C-130A aircraft. Later, improvements included 4-bladed propellers from another manufacturer, designated C-130B models.

A different letter suffix is used for each aircraft model to denote major changes to the airframe and/or systems. Many years later, a more powerful engine and five-bladed propellers were installed, giving rise to the C-130J.

The C-130 is the most versatile aircraft in the world. It can land on paved runways, dirt strips, snow, and even water. Remarkably, about forty unassisted takeoffs and landings were made on the aircraft carrier USS Forrestal. Today, more than seventy countries operate either the C-130 or its commercial version, the L-100, or both. It would likely take a full college term just to cover the traits, merits, conversions, models, and accomplishments of the C-130

Hercules—and that still wouldn't be adequate for all the details.

The U.S. military needed a new type of aircraft to train jet pilots, and four major manufacturers were selected to design and build prototypes to compete. I understood that a four-engine design was preferred. Each time Lockheed developed a new aircraft, employees were encouraged to submit name suggestions. The winner received a $500 bond. I submitted "Southern Star," but "JetStar" was chosen. I tied for third place, which meant nothing. Lockheed built the four-engine JetStar and won the "fly-off" competition, but the Air Force ultimately decided it needed a two-engine trainer.

Lockheed-Georgia manufactured several JetStars for executive use. Howard Hughes—a business magnate, investor, record-setting pilot, engineer, film director, and one of the most financially successful people of his time—bought several. He rented ramp space to park them and hired guards. Whenever a company wanted a JetStar quickly, he had them available for immediate sale. When he sold one, he ordered another.

Lockheed was selected to design and build the world's largest military aircraft. Another employee and I submitted the name "Galaxy," which won. He received the $500 first prize, while I was given an engraved cigarette lighter and "honorable mention." Guess which I preferred—I didn't even smoke! (This was before tobacco had a bad reputation.)

The C-5 Galaxy features truck-bed-height loading, similar to the C-130. This means a truck can back up and unload cargo directly into the aircraft. The cargo compartment is so large

Lockheed Employment – 1961-1963

that an eight-lane bowling alley would fit inside. The first flight by the Wright Brothers was shorter than the length of the C-5's interior. It can hold fifty-eight Cadillacs or six standard Greyhound buses. The nose swivels upward, and rear doors swing outward, allowing a large truck to drive through the front or rear, unload cargo, and exit the other end. The main landing gear has twenty-four tires, and the nose gear has four, all the same size. It is a fantastic aircraft.

During my career with Lockheed-Georgia, the company built B-47s, C-130s, C-141s, C-5s, and JetStars. The Lockheed California Company in Burbank simultaneously built several other aircraft, including the SR-71 Blackbird, L-1011 TriStar, and P-3 Orion. The SR-71 was a super-secret spy plane capable of flying faster and higher than any other aircraft, with cameras that could photograph a car's license plate from altitude. Its published speed was 2,200 mph, but I'm sure it was faster. Incidentally, Lockheed Martin (after Lockheed and Martin merged) reportedly unveiled the SR-72 hypersonic scramjet spy plane in 2013. This unmanned aircraft, successor to the SR-71, is capable of speeds over 4,500 mph.

As far as I know, every aircraft built by Lockheed was designed by Kelly Johnson and his engineering team at the Lockheed Skunk Works in Burbank, California. He was a superior design engineer, and the aircraft I've mentioned are just a portion of those credited to Skunk Works. (As I mentioned before, the B-47 was designed by Boeing or at least Boeing was the prime manufacturer.)

I continued working on B-47 aircraft on the flight line, represented hourly workers as union Senior Chairman, attended college five days a week, and spent time with Ricky. I would have been laid off around 1958 if I hadn't accepted the union position.

In 1961, the flight line foreman told me there was an opening in the Field Service Department and suggested it would be a good opportunity. This was a salaried job, paying more than hourly positions, with excellent travel opportunities representing Lockheed-Georgia to customers who purchased Lockheed aircraft. I didn't want to go overseas, but C-130s were operated by the U.S. Air Force, Navy, Marines, and soon by the Air Force Reserve and National Guard.

All I needed was to score at least 110 on the Management Selection Exam (an IQ test) and pass an interview with the Field Service Department manager. The flight line hourly workers tried to dissuade me, but I explained I hadn't spent so much time in college to continue working hourly. Some didn't understand my logic.

I took the exam, passed with a good grade, and was accepted into Field Service. I went from one of the highest hourly grades to Salary Grade Six with a handshake.

(A few years later, I was told Lockheed could no longer require a written exam for Field Service jobs because it was discriminatory. I never quite understood why.)

I had to quit college because I was assigned to a C-130 aircraft school for several months but felt confident I would return to college soon since I had no plans to go overseas.

That, however, was make-believe!

Chapter 4
Lockheed Employment - 1961-63

I'm unsure of the exact date I took the test and transferred to Field Service, but I believe it was around September 1, 1961. I was immediately introduced to everyone in the office and the "Reps" who were either between assignments or newly hired. At that time, there were only a small number of Field Service Representatives. Getting to know one another and hearing the tall tales from those who had already been on assignment was very interesting.

In those days, it was mandatory to wear a nice, dark business suit, dark socks matching the suit, a very conservative tie, and dark business shoes. The dress code was clear: either look like a Wall Street banker or find another job.

The Vice President of Marketing and Product Support spent a long time briefing us on the dos and don'ts. (Several years later, I would report directly to him.) We attended a C-130 school taught by Field Service Training Department personnel. Most classes were general, since each aircraft series had various improvements or system changes. The school lasted about four months.

After completing the school, I worked with the office team that proofread all reports from the Reps on assignment and forwarded copies to numerous Lockheed-Georgia divisions—engineering, marketing, top management, and others. This group also handled inquiries from Field Service Reps, obtaining necessary information from responsible departments to answer questions. I learned a great deal about technical writing and the kind of reports I would have to produce on assignment.

Altogether, I almost felt like I was on vacation—no college work and no union duties. I was able to spend more time with Ricky, who celebrated his fifth birthday on February 23, 1962. As soon as I could afford it, I bought two lots in a Marietta subdivision and had a nice three-bedroom, three-bath brick house built to ensure Ricky would have a decent place to live. The house also had a two-car garage and a daylight basement.

I was getting used to dressing like a banker and carrying a briefcase. The definition of an expert is "a man (or woman) fifty miles from home with a briefcase," so I now needed to be fifty miles from home. I was sorely afraid it would be much farther when I was sent on assignment.

Around March 1962, my boss told me to pack up and leave for Albany, Georgia, as I would be assigned to Turner Air Force Base until further notice. Wow, I thought, "Throw me in that briar patch any time." God had answered my prayers. Turner AFB was roughly two hundred miles from Marietta and less than fifty miles from my parents' farm. I could see everyone frequently.

Two men were currently assigned to Turner, and I would replace one while the other remained. The one I would work with, Charlie, had been an electronics supervisor on the flight line a few years prior. He was a very nice person, and I was even more eager to take the assignment. I felt sorry for the Rep leaving, as he wanted to stay there forever.

Lockheed Employment – 1961-1963

I rented a very nice, new duplex with excellent furnishings and great soundproofing. I felt so blessed! My parents wasted no time visiting and were excited to have me close to "home."

Turner AFB was home to a squadron of C-130A aircraft used for photo mapping worldwide. They were currently mapping South America, with some aircraft temporarily based in about three countries there.

Charlie, the senior Rep in our group, covered C-130 avionics systems; a representative from Allison handled engine issues; a Hamilton Standard rep took care of propellers; and I was responsible for the rest of the aircraft. All four of us shared an office, so I met them upon arrival. I was then introduced to the Air Base Director of Maintenance, numerous USAF maintenance officials, pilots, and others.

Acting on the "theory" that an expert is a person carrying a briefcase fifty miles from home, I flashed my brand-new, dust-free briefcase and set about proving the theory. Everyone always has questions, and I have another theory: "If they ask the right questions, I have the right answers." I never tried to bluff; if I didn't know the answer, I promised to find it. I found that customer personnel worldwide appreciate someone who is always available and eager to help. A Lockheed Field Service Rep was supposed to provide information and not get physically involved—because of insurance and liability issues—though sometimes you just have to touch things.

Charlie's wife had been paralyzed shortly before I arrived. She became paralyzed from the waist down and was virtually homebound. When Lockheed sent people on assignment, they were expected to be available to assist customers 24 hours a day, seven days a week. I volunteered to cover nights and weekends whenever possible so Charlie could be home with his wife. Of course, I hoped to see Ricky and my parents occasionally as well.

Charlie and his wife often invited me for dinner, followed by a few games of chess with him. These evenings helped break up their sense that the walls were closing in. I respected Charlie's knowledge of electronics and felt I could learn a great deal about field assignments from him. We spent considerable time discussing C-130 systems, including radar, radios, navigation, and more. He knew I had been an electrician but was majoring in physics with a heavy focus on electronics. I understood electronics but had never worked directly with C-130 avionics.

A few months after I arrived at Turner AFB, one of the squadron's C-130A aircraft suffered a nose landing gear failure while landing at Georgetown, British Guiana (now Guyana). The aircraft's nose skidded on the runway, causing some structural damage. I was dispatched to advise the mechanics on a temporary repair so the aircraft could be flown back to the U.S. for permanent repairs. I packed a suitcase, grabbed my briefcase (to prove I was an "expert"), and was flown there on another squadron C-130. I felt confident because the Lockheed Field Service technical support group and company engineers stood ready to provide information as needed.

Upon arrival at the small airbase on Georgetown's outskirts, I was briefed on the incident and then inspected the aircraft,

Lockheed Employment – 1961-1963

which had been towed to the parking ramp. Of course, I carried my briefcase to ensure no one doubted my expertise. After thoroughly assessing the damage, I called Lockheed and provided my contacts with a list of damaged components and my assessment of the nose gear failure's cause. We communicated back and forth for several days as engineers prepared detailed instructions for a temporary repair. Once I received the engineering data, I passed it to the mechanics, who carried out the work. I stayed with them most of the time to observe and answer questions.

I was advised that demonstrations were occurring in Georgetown and much of the city had been burned as the people sought independence from England. Therefore, I spent very little time in town. The country had been colonized by England, as had the U.S., but eventually the British relented and granted freedom.

From 1954 to 2010, as I traveled worldwide, numerous countries broke away from various European "masters" who had claimed them as colonies. Some people joked that a "wake of problems" followed me to many places, but that was coincidental—I pray no one truly believed I was a jinx.

I met a family that owned the largest hydroponics garden in the world—or at least the largest in South America. I was told the U.S. government built it during WWII to provide fresh vegetables and fruit to troops in the region. I toured the garden and was amazed by its size and the quality and quantity of produce. Some U.S. officers at the airbase and I invited the owner and his wife to the small officers' club for grilled steaks. They brought fresh corn, potatoes, and tomatoes to accompany the meal, and the taste was fantastic.

(No, this did not interfere with my job.) Developing a hydroponics garden, even on a smaller scale, would be expensive but less labor-intensive for producing fruits and vegetables.

As the C-130A's temporary repair progressed, three officers suggested renting a small boat to go fishing upriver (I don't recall the river's name). We donated blood to the local mosquitoes despite using repellent, but those were the only bites we suffered—no fish. The views of wildflowers, butterflies, and the surrounding nature made the trip worthwhile. A couple of us removed our shoes and dangled our bare feet in the water as the boat cruised along, hoping for relief from the heat and humidity—until someone warned we might be trolling for crocodiles and piranhas. We withdrew our feet immediately!

About two weeks after arriving, the temporary repairs were completed. I instructed the mechanics to remove the nose landing gear doors and showed them how to secure the nose gear in the down position, as it was unstable due to damage. The flight crew was advised that the aircraft would have to fly back to Albany with the nose gear extended and the cabin unpressurized, requiring flight below 10,000 feet and at lower airspeeds—thus consuming more fuel. Given these constraints, the crew decided to stop in San Juan, Puerto Rico, to check for wind buffeting damage inside the nose gear wheel well and to refuel. We spent less than 24 hours in San Juan. The complete trip from Georgetown to Albany, Georgia, was trouble-free.

The entire South America trip lasted less than three weeks, but I felt I had done my duty by traveling overseas! I was

Lockheed Employment – 1961-1963

eager to make another trip—this time to Marietta to see Ricky and to the farm to visit my parents.

It took three phone calls to the Marietta office to provide details of the temporary repair job. I hoped a star would be placed beside my name.

As time passed, I grew fonder of my assignment and wanted to stay there forever—reminding me of my predecessor at Turner AFB, who had said the same.

Jed Walker, my former supervisor in Engineering Flight Test who had transferred to Field Service, had recently returned from an assignment in Indonesia and was now the manager. I knew he was sharp.

I was inwardly smiling, having been on this assignment for a year, when the office telephone rang. I picked it up and was surprised to hear Jed's voice. We exchanged the usual pleasantries, then he said, "Bill, how would you like to go to Indonesia on an assignment to set up and teach a specialist class on all the C-130 avionics systems?" I replied, "No, thank you. Remember, I'm an electrician. I don't even know where Indonesia is. I'm happy here." He said, "I'm aware of your college education in electronic physics, so it will be a snap for you." (I assumed the "snap" would be my neck when I was hung.) "You're the only person we have for this job. Will you do it?" With no real choice, I agreed.

On the Lockheed flight line, technicians specialized in radar, navigation systems, radios, and other areas. None of the specialists I knew crossed those lines, although an avionics field service rep was expected to do so. Now, there were no lines for me—about fifteen avionics systems to teach in depth to people with limited English, some of whom were expected to teach these highly technical systems after attending my school. I was no longer smiling—just thinking, "Woe is me!"

I went around to say goodbye to the Air Force personnel and civilians, loaded my clothes into the car, and headed for Lockheed in Marietta, reminding myself that "grown men don't cry" (especially when people are watching).

After arriving at Lockheed, I spent several days undergoing a physical examination, receiving what felt like every immunization shot ever invented to update my international vaccine record, and being briefed on the trip to Indonesia. I would be part of a five-man team tasked with teaching the entire C-130 aircraft. We were told to dress casually and for the heat—no suits or ties—because the country had limited air conditioning, even though Jakarta, where we would be based, lies only four degrees south of the equator.

We could expect to be on this assignment for six months under a U.S. Military Advisor Contract (later extended to fifteen months), allowing us to purchase products at the U.S. Government commissary and live as if we were at home. Ha.

We were now as ready to depart as possible. I had forgotten how to smile. I was leaving Ricky and my parents behind and remained deeply concerned about the courses I would have to teach.

Chapter 5
Indonesia - 1962-1963

We stopped at Clark Air Base near Manila, Philippines, where General MacArthur had his office during World War II. My brother Milford was killed near the city of Cebu on Cebu Island, but we didn't have enough time for me to fly there. The base commander handed us the keys to a jeep and local road maps filled with information about buildings, restaurants, sightseeing, and more. We had a great time for ten days before he boarded us on a plane that took our team to Jakarta, Indonesia—a very large city.

Indonesia is an archipelago of about twenty thousand islands. The country is rich in minerals, oil, natural gas, rice plantations, coffee, tea, spices, and many other resources. Sukarno had overthrown the president, taken control, and appointed a cabinet that made him president for life. They embezzled the country's wealth to purchase Russian MIG fighters, cargo aircraft, trucks, jeeps, and more. The currency plummeted from seventy to ten thousand Rials per US dollar. Merchants were required to buy dollars from banks to import goods, which was impossible, forcing many to close their businesses. The only way to purchase goods was through the black market.

The US began providing food, clothing, and other aid, but the Russians controlled the harbors, warehouses, and distribution. When shipments arrived for Indonesian civilians, the Russians removed the original labels and replaced them with their own, diverting goods to the black market. Sukarno and his Russian allies controlled this illicit trade. Meanwhile, the population starved as rice paddies, spice farms, and lush fields were abandoned.

The US government donated several C-130 aircraft to help transport goods across the islands, which was beneficial, but there was little food to move beyond small farms. The turbines on the hydroelectric generators were worn out, leaving Jakarta with limited water and power—no air conditioning. The city lies about four degrees south of the equator, making it tropical with two seasons: hot and dry, followed by a monsoon season far more intense than most Americans can imagine.

Our embassy had secured a large two-story house with spacious apartments upstairs and downstairs. Jim and I took the upstairs unit, while the other three team members occupied the lower floor. Directly across the street was the country's largest mosque, where we were serenaded five times a day, seven days a week, by loudspeakers mounted on the roof. The call to prayer was broadcast so loudly it could be heard throughout the neighborhood. I assumed the residents either prayed in silence or slept through it. The first prayer was around dusk, and the next at about 5 a.m. My alarm clock was never needed after that. A man shouted the prayers into a microphone, and since our windows were never closed—there was no air conditioning—the sound permeated the apartments.

Our new home was well equipped, including enough food to last a week. The first thing we did was hire a cook and cleaner for each apartment. They were starving and willing to work for nothing, but we paid them well and allowed their

Indonesia – 1962-63

families to move in. There were two large servant quarters and a two-car enclosed garage. The servants would never own a car, but I was able to purchase a nice British sedan that the embassy had brought into Indonesia. The embassy issued us a large Russian jeep, which we all used. I was the only instructor with a personal vehicle, which I kept locked in the garage unless I wanted to go somewhere alone or have the servants wash and polish it. It still looked new when I left fifteen months later.

We took the Russian jeep to the embassy to exchange money for Indonesian Rupiah, then to the embassy store where US goods could be purchased with dollars. The next day, we met the Ambassador and the US military commander at the embassy. They briefed us on the country and explained why Lockheed had been contracted to pay for our services. The US military also provided training manuals and "viewers" for classroom use. The head of missions was introduced—a handsome man who looked more like a professional tennis player than a diplomat. I knew that a CIA agent was always present in every embassy, often disguised as an agriculture advisor or mission officers. When he began speaking, we exchanged knowing glances that lasted several seconds. I realized he was in total control of the embassy and all US operations in the country. I had no idea how many agents he commanded.

The following Monday, we set up our classrooms and began teaching. I had an ideal group of twelve students, all with basic electronics training. One had experience repairing C-130 aircraft radios and was the only fluent English speaker, so he was selected as my interpreter. Some students would become teachers in civilian schools, while others would train Air Force personnel. I had fifteen months to teach them the details of fourteen complex avionics systems. I wished I were back on the farm with Ricky and Mama, but I had an assignment to complete, so I focused on the program.

I had always wanted to sing or play an instrument but never had encouragement. This seemed far enough from home to give it a try. My condo mate, Jim, spoke a few words of Indonesian and surprised me when he found a Chinese man in Jakarta who taught classical Spanish guitar lessons and encouraged me to learn. Jim was very musical but had never mastered the Spanish guitar, his favorite instrument. The only sounds we heard were the calls to prayer from the mosque across the street. After three weeks of lessons, my tutor told me not to return because he couldn't teach me anymore. Jim had already hinted that he couldn't continue either. Putting those clues together, I knew my musical career was over.

There was a country club with a nice golf course a short distance from our classrooms, and the embassy had secured permission for us to join. Two of the instructors were avid golfers, but I had only played once before. They encouraged me to join, so we stopped by the club and signed up. I asked if I could rent a set of clubs; they had only one set available, which I was allowed to purchase. It should have been scrapped ten years earlier.

Mr. Riding, who had been my supervisor during the C-130 engineering flight test and later as manager of customer service, called to check if I was pleased with my job. I'm sure he already knew the answer, so I asked how things were

Indonesia – 1962-63

going. He said he had been promoted to manager of C-130 sales in the Far East and was planning a trip to Indonesia. He wondered if he could bring me anything. I said, "You threw me into this briar patch, so I'd appreciate it if you'd buy top-of-the-line golf clubs and a bag, plus golf shoes, gloves, six dozen golf balls, and a bag of tees." He laughed and said he'd be happy to do that in Hong Kong, but it would still be expensive. I told him I'd already played two rounds and planned to be a champion. He arrived with much better equipment than I imagined—better than anything at the golf course, including what the professional golfers used. My caddie had a three handicap, and the number one pro played with my threesome at least three times a week. I played eighteen to thirty-six holes daily, seven days a week. At that time, golf carts were only in the USA, so I walked several miles every day for about fifteen months.

About two weeks after settling in, I drove to Hotel Indonesia to have a milkshake—the only place to get one. I sat at a small table in the corner, sipping my shake and studying radar system diagrams. Suddenly, it got quiet, and I noticed every eye was on the front door. I looked and saw the most beautiful girl in the world heading my way. I focused on her until she stopped and asked if it would bother me if she sat down and had a milkshake too. I replied that I'd be very bothered but honored. She told the waiter to bring a shake just like mine. We talked for three hours. I asked why a beautiful girl like her would sit with someone like me. She said I was handsome and that she realized I was a little older, but that didn't bother her. I discovered I was thirteen years older. She said, "I came here to have a milkshake, but I saw you and decided to have one with you. I hope I haven't offended you." I said I wasn't offended but wanted to know why she chose me. She said she and her mother had been invited to a US Embassy affair, where the Ambassador introduced us to Mr. Riding. Mr. Riding said, "I know Nina isn't allowed to date anyone, but you must meet Bill Walls. He's a very nice, genius electronics engineer." He even gave us your picture, which I kept so I'd recognize you. I just want to know you better." I said, "I'm not young, handsome, very nice, or a genius." She said I was too modest and believed Mr. Riding. She had been there too long, so she asked if I had swimming shorts and would like to meet for a swim the next morning. I had two new pairs but couldn't use the pool. She said she hadn't seen the pool but was sure they'd let us use it. She briefly touched my hand and dashed for the door. Two bodyguards rose from a table and followed her; two held the door open, and her car door was open.

Everything went well for thirteen months, but I decided to end it before it went too far. The most beautiful and wealthiest woman in the world and I were deeply in love. Her mother told me Nina would inherit her money when she died. I said I had worked hard and never accepted charity. She said this wasn't charity; Nina had inherited the money. "You and Nina are in love, and if you marry her, you can buy anything you want. If you find her unattractive, I will understand. But if you still reject her, you are too proud, arrogant, and stupid." She went to another room and closed the door. I sat beside Nina, but she said, "I know you had a bad marriage and vowed never to marry again. We are deeply in love, so this will be perfect. Ricky can live with us and share in our perfect love." Both of us cried, knowing what was coming. She wouldn't even let me touch her hand. She

Indonesia – 1962-63

finally stopped crying and asked me to lock the door behind me. When I did, I knew I would never open it again. I had hurt three people, and the only consolation was my belief that they now knew Jesus Christ. If so, I hoped to see them again. I remain very sad but strive to glorify Christ. I don't know why it ended this way, but I pray my Savior approves.

All my team and the Lockheed reps at the airbase drank heavily. Knowing I was a Christian, I was never asked to join. On my thirtieth birthday, they threw me a surprise party. The only drinks were iced tea and Coke. I was shocked and asked why. They said they were "off the wagon." I prayed they stayed that way.

I studied avionics systems every night to teach well the next day. After about twenty minutes of teaching, I had my interpreter repeat everything because the class struggled with my South Georgia accent. Everyone in South Georgia had the same problem, and Yankees found it impossible. That didn't bother me—we had to play the cards we were dealt.

Two weeks before Christmas, the Indonesian officer gathered the five of us and said, "Our government appreciates your work and would like to send you on a two-week, all-expenses-paid vacation to Bali." One teammate had brought his wife and declined. Another was a "deadhead" from California who seemed lost and unaware of his surroundings; he also declined. The other three of us accepted joyfully. At some point, Bob Hope starred in the movie On the Road to Bali. I thought that was Hollywood fiction—now I had a chance to see it. I was ready to pack, but we had to work two more weeks of golf and teaching. Such suffering I had.

We finally boarded a two-engine propeller plane, signaling a rough ride—rougher than I imagined—but we didn't complain.

An army captain drove us to the best hotel on the island, a single-story motel with no air conditioning. The windows never closed. The tile roof was designed to keep rooms cool by not absorbing heat, allowing a gentle breeze inside. The mosquitoes were huge and fierce, entering through the open windows twenty-four hours a day. Thankfully, large mosquito nets hung from ceiling to floor around the beds, keeping mosquitoes out. The downside was that mosquitoes were already inside, and the nets were raised for a couple of hours each morning to trap any new arrivals. Our bedding and clothes were soaked with blood, but we didn't complain—just happy to have donated a lot of blood to the Indonesian Red Cross.

The captain picked us up at seven a.m. since the motel had no restaurant. We bought all his meals and gave him a generous tip every day—considerably more than the army paid him. Each meal, we went to a different Polynesian restaurant, and the food was always excellent.

At that time, most of Indonesia was moderately Muslim, allowing freedom of religion, while Bali was predominantly Hindu. Indonesia was engaged in a conflict with the Netherlands, trying to incorporate the Dutch East Indies into Indonesia. Dutch forces were dropping paratroopers into the jungles. Someone akin to Jimmy Carter pressured the Dutch

Indonesia – 1962-63

to withdraw and let Indonesia take control. Our president likely received substantial funding for another aid program.

Sorry for the sidetrack, but that had to be said! In Bali, every woman, from birth until death, wears a Bali blouse—meaning a grass skirt and nothing else. No one is allowed to stare or take photographs. On our last Saturday night there, the captain took us to a village deep in the jungle. He said, "The natives are having a big party tonight, and the chief has allowed us to attend." We had already been told not to bring cameras.

Indonesia is home to very exotic birds, butterflies, and numerous animals, and it seems even more beautiful than Polynesia. I never saw any cages. Indonesia boasts more than 250 castles—far more than any other country. The village had no castle, just sheer natural beauty. We parked and looked around. There was a large depression about five feet deep with a gentle upward slope all around, forming a perfect amphitheater. The acoustics were unbelievable. Numerous bonfires surrounded the area, with people cooking on all of them. No other lights or buildings were in sight—just beautiful flowers and grass. I didn't see any chairs, tables, or cutlery.

A man approached and told us to follow him, which we did. All the men were seated single file down the slope, with the chief in the center, illuminated by two spotlights on each side. I was to sit on one side of the chief, and Jim on the other. We prepared to sit on the ground, but a man suddenly appeared with a chair and placed it in my spot. I shook my head and pointed to the chief, but he simply said, "Please sit." It sounded more like a command than a request. I felt like a target but sat down. I had an unobstructed view of the flowers and butterflies. I stared at them, not at the beautiful girls wearing Bali blouses and grass skirts. All had copper skin and wavy black hair. I was a Christian and felt I shouldn't be there, but I prayed that God would understand.

Each woman walked around carrying a plate of peeled fruit and a small glass of juice. Each stopped in front of a man and handed him the plate and glass. I closed my eyes so I wouldn't stare. As a born blinker, I had a close view of a beautiful young girl, about eighteen, well-endowed and wearing a stunning Bali blouse. She smiled and handed me the plate and glass. I prayed for God's blessing on the food. No one knew what I said, as they worship many gods. The older women collected the plates and glasses and returned to the other side.

Meanwhile, the girls gathered in the depression. Some sang while others danced gracefully like ballerinas. The young girl who had served me glided up the slope and grasped my hands. I glanced at the village chief, who said, "You must dance with her, or she and I will be shamed." I certainly didn't want to bring shame upon them. I had taken ballroom dance lessons but wasn't good. She was fantastic—I never stepped on her bare feet. Everyone gave us a standing ovation, which I knew was for her. She gave me a quick kiss and glided away.

When I sat down, the chief said, "That was a Jogot Boom Boom, the dance of love. Now you are married and must take her with you." I said, "If I must, I will bear the stripes." He and everyone around us burst into laughter. I asked what was so funny. He said he was joking. I already knew that if we

Indonesia – 1962-63

were married, I'd have to live on the island with beautiful Bali blouses. Most of the world has never seen such a work of art; what I saw was the best of the best.

One night, Jim and I were sitting in our living room when we heard a lot of noise. Looking toward the mosque, we saw an enormous mob filling the streets and sidewalks in all directions. Unless you were there, you wouldn't believe the scene. It was possible that a million or more people were in this uncontrolled mob. Mobs had been killing Chinese and other nationals for weeks because President Sukarno blamed them for the food shortages in Indonesia.

I believe in getting in touch with God, so I started praying. Suddenly, there was a knock on the door, and our cook entered with Indonesians behind her. She was trying to prove we were Americans, not British, so they wanted to see our identification. Jim and I handed her our open passports. The leaders said, "Americans are good, British are bad," and left. We gave the cook a large box full of Rials for saving our lives.

When John F. Kennedy was assassinated, Pete Seota, the Indonesian harbor master, came to our house in tears. He was very tall and muscular, so I couldn't imagine him crying over anything. We hadn't heard the news due to the twenty-three-hour, thirty-minute time difference between Atlanta and Indonesia. Pete told us about the killing and then about his day. A large Russian ship had docked, and his crew boarded to check the manifest before allowing them ashore. The captain refused inspection, so Pete picked him up and threw him into the water. He then found many expensive, undeclared items on board. I was sure Pete took most of the cargo home.

Sometime later, I was back home with Ricky and my parents for four weeks. Mama had named Ricky and probably loved him more than me. That was okay. She always had a big pot of his favorite vegetable soup when he arrived. The four of us were the happiest we had ever been, and I again considered resigning from Lockheed. But I knew I would never earn enough money to give Ricky a better life. I knew the best life for all of us would be on the farm. I made the wrong decision and accepted an assignment in Pakistan. Woe is me!

Chapter 6
Pakistan - 1963-1964

Lockheed officials told me to stop in Wiesbaden, Germany, for a briefing by a USAF Colonel, so I checked into a nearby hotel where Lockheed had made reservations for me.

The next day, I called his office and identified myself. The receptionist said that he would like to see me, but he was out of town for a few days. She said, "Give me your telephone number and see the sites. He will call you," so I did.

Four days later, the colonel called and asked if I could come over for a short meeting. It was nearby, so I called a taxi and zipped over. When I walked in, I saw the receptionist and several offices with the doors closed. She asked if I was Mr. Walls, and I said, "Mr. Walls was my father; I am William Walls". I saw that she was confused, so I apologized and told her that I was from South Georgia. She just shook her head and buzzed the colonel, then pointed to the office across from her. I assumed that she did not understand South Georgia English. No wonder my brothers didn't take long to conquer Germany.

The colonel did not know anything about Pakistan but insisted that I stop on the way back home for a debriefing. This was indeed strange that someone in charge of a six to eight million dollars a year aid program didn't know anything about the country that was receiving it.

The next day, I flew to Karachi, Pakistan, and checked into a dingy hotel which was about two blocks north of the

Arabian Sea. My room was on the second floor with a six-lane street out front. I had a close-up and personal relationship with the scenery outside. At least fourteen hours daily, there was a steady stream of bullock or camel caravans going about one kilometer per hour, all dropping large clumps of dung. As soon as the traffic slowed, a multitude of women and girls dashed out and cleared the streets of the fresh dung. This was put into homemade carts or woven reed baskets which were placed on top of the heads of the women and girls. This seeped into their hair and clothing; very repulsive and unthinkable in the Western world. The married women are forced to wear a veil and burqa. If another man other than their husband sees any part of the body, even by accident, the husband is authorized to kill her anyway he wants. This is also condoned if any other of his family shames him by leaving Islam or dating anyone without his permission. This is Sharia law. Islam was founded by Prophet Muhammad late in the fifth century AD in Mecca, Saudi Arabia. He was a member of the Quraish tribe, the most powerful trading company. Muhammad somehow believed that he was the messiah! Why? India was one country of the British Empire. The USA, Bermuda, and several other countries in North America, Central America, South America, Europe, Africa, Asia, and Australasia covered areas around the world, so the sun never set on the British Empire. In 1947, the Indians were attacking the British and others to drive them out, so the country was split into three parts: East Pakistan, West Pakistan, and India in the middle. India was primarily Hindu, and the others were primarily Muslim, but there were still mixtures in all three.

Pakistan – 1963-1964

After watching the sights in Karachi for two days, I boarded a USAF cargo airplane of WWII vintage. I was very happy to be flying to Rawalpindi, Pakistan, because the air in Karachi was hot, humid, and had a horrible stench of dung and unwashed bodies, plus many other things. Nothing could be worse. Wrong again! When I went down a step ladder onto the tarmac of Rawalpindi Airport, I thought, "Why me, Lord? Mama, come get me and take me home!". I was ready to pick cotton and fight the gnats in one hundred degrees plus weather. It got worse when the Lockheed Representative grasped my hand and said, "Let me take you home". I had just asked mama to take me home. Home was only a short distance from the airport. It looked like a small one-story motel with ten rooms. My room was on one end of the row, with excellent air conditioning, a large bedroom, bathroom, and large room behind with a two-door clothes closet, chest of drawers, and much more. A much larger building was about forty feet away. Ron Dennis was the Lockheed Rep who covered the mechanical part of the C-130 aircraft, and I would handle the electronics. He was the person who was showing me around; I saw that he was congenial, so we would work well together. We headed over to see the lounge room, kitchen, and dining room; each was very large. The cook was a US Army Master Sergeant, but he would only cook in an emergency. He had hired a cook and three waiters and would plan menus, fly to the USAF air base in Peshawar, Pakistan, in the northern area of the country. There was a PX and commissary there where he purchased all of the food supplies. I met the other three representatives: one from Allison Division of General Motors, who built C-130 engines; the next rep was from Hamilton Standard, manufacturer of C-130 propellers; and the other rep was from a helicopter manufacturer. Life was looking better. Our home had been recently built using US aid funds. The name of it was "Pindi Palace". I couldn't help wondering how long it would be before our social security and Medicaid funds were depleted.

The next morning, we went through a small gate that was an entrance to the Pakistan Air Force Base. This was a short walk from airport check-in. The air force maintenance director was a one-eyed colonel. After a short chat, we made a tour around the flight line and maintenance shops; the last was the electronics shop. I spent the rest of the morning trying to train the technicians, but each of them wanted me to help them with various problems at the same time. All of the Reps walked back to Pindi Palace for a very good lunch and an hour rest, then back to work. Electronics was always the hardest subject to get across, especially if there was a language problem. There were a multitude of problems in this case. In order to protect the innocent, I won't continue. The technicians came and knocked hard on my door twenty-four hours a day, seven days a week.

About two weeks later, I had to hide out somewhere for a quick break, so I walked over to the Pakistan Air Line building and sat down at a small table. I saw a nice-looking young woman wearing a PIA hostess uniform walking by. We both said, "Hi," but she didn't slow down. I drank a slightly warm coke and then went back to my impossible task. As we were having dinner, I mentioned my encounter at the airport. Everyone seemed to know the young woman

Pakistan – 1963-1964

and informed me that she was dating a PIA pilot and singing with a band at night. She supposedly was also dating a band member. I knew I could never get into something like that, so I just erased everything from my mind.

A few weeks later, the army sergeant had invited about eight people for dinner. I was sitting on the center cushion of a sofa in the lounge when the guests arrived. I was the only person that didn't know anyone, and people tried not to see me, so I didn't get up. There seemed to be a bit of hustle and bustle going on, so I leaned back when two girls sat down beside me. The one on my left was the one I had met at the airport. They asked for my name, and I replied, so I asked for their information. The one from the airport said that her name was Valerie Brady, and she remembered me from the airport. The other one lived at Mangla Dam with her mother and father, both of whom were with her now. They were from the USA. She was seventeen years old, and Valerie was nineteen. I was twelve years older than Valerie and fourteen years older than the other one. I knew they were kids, so I stood up to meet the other guests. Then everyone went in for dinner. One of the waiters came around for drink orders, and the other was bringing large dishes of meat and vegetables, which he placed along the center, giving access for each person without passing dishes. I ordered a coke, and everyone else had wine. Dessert was brought in after the main course. All of the food was good as always, so I decided that was the only thing good in Pakistan, and I still believe that sixty years later.

At some time, Valerie and I met at a party, and we talked more. She was born in India in 1945. Her father's name was

Major Cliff Brady, who was born in Canada and moved to Jersey, a small island near France. He then joined the British Army when he was fourteen as a boot cleaner and tea maker, and worked up to the rank of major in World War Two. He was transferred to India where he met Valerie's mother when she was attending school at a Catholic Convent. Her mother's family had been in India for several generations, and I assumed they had married Indians since they no longer had citizenship anywhere. Cliff and Erin married, then Valerie and one of her sisters were born. The Indians started a revolt to drive the British out. In 1947, India was divided into three countries: West Pakistan and East Pakistan, with India in the middle. The Brady family moved to West Pakistan.

We met at another party about a month later. She asked whether I had eaten curry, which I had not, so we made a date to have curry in Rawalpindi. That was the best food that I had ever eaten. Muslim countries do not eat pork, so the restaurants only offer chicken, lamb, beef, goat, fish, or vegetables. Indians worship almost everything; therefore, they are vegetarian but will cook chickens for foreigners. Curry originated in India when salt was unavailable, so they put about twenty spices in the food so the lack of salt would not be noticed. Mild curry has a few pieces of red pepper, and if people want it hotter, more red peppers are added. The hottest is Vindaloo, my favorite, but few people agree because their bodies cannot handle the red peppers. I had just found the second good thing about India. Since I was in a good mood for a change, Valerie wanted me to meet her family. I drove a short distance and met her father and mother, Cliff and Erin, and her brothers, Chris and Roger

Pakistan – 1963-1964

Brady. A charming family, and Roger shared my sense of humor.

On my next monthly shopping trip to the USAF Air Base in Peshawar, I remembered that Gary Powers had flown the Lockheed U2 spy aircraft out of this base over Russia until a Russian missile damaged the aircraft, forcing Gary to land and be captured. The Russians held him and the aircraft until the KGB proved that this was a spy aircraft and Gary Powers was a taxi driver; oh no, a SPY! It bothered me when I found that the KGB might have attended the same sleuth school as our CIA. Such a deduction! I knew that the U2 could fly for hours at altitudes over seventy thousand feet, and the cameras could photograph a license plate. No aircraft or missile could reach sixty thousand feet. The USA had to pay a ton of gold for the release of Gary, but the KGB kept the aircraft so their experts could reverse engineer it. Gary was never of interest to them, just the aircraft. Another generous aid program to our worst enemy. Being very nosy, I felt that I must investigate. All I had to do to get an audience with the men that serviced the U2 was flash my ID card. They told me that someone had bribed the Pakistani man who serviced the oxygen system to loosen a nut that would allow oxygen to bleed out. When the oxygen was depleted, Gary had to make a rapid descent to about twenty thousand feet in order to live. Several MIG fighters surrounded him, forcing him to land. The KGB had captured him and the U2 without firing a shot. As far as I know, this was never released to the public because it would have shamed the CIA. Woe is us.

Valerie asked me if I would like to celebrate New Year's night at a black-tie affair in the nightclub. I said, "No. I don't have a tuxedo; I don't like to dance, and I understand that you are dating a member of the band". She said that was not the truth. I couldn't help but ponder this, but finally agreed to go. Then I had to hire a tailor to make a tuxedo and all of the complements. She wore an Indian Sari, much nicer than an evening gown, which looked great on her. Later, Valerie led me onto the dance floor; I almost forgot about the bad music from the band. We ended the night about sunup the next morning.

I was unable to make anyone understand that they could not continue waking me every night and come to my home any hour on the weekends and ask me to go to the base to solve problems for them, so Val and her parents found a house in a small village that was for rent shortly after the first of January 1964. It had no heat, no A/C, no water heater, and no furniture. Housing and wood were extremely scarce. This was standard housing for the few people with good jobs. The next step down had mud huts. The other people had caves, which were full, or a spot on the ground until the owner of the spot "cleared" the area. Anyway, I rented it for too much money and bought furniture, table lamps, two small kerosene space heaters, and the other items that were needed. Then I took a flight on the Pakistan Air flight to Peshawar to purchase a ton of stuff from the US Military PX and commissary. When I got back to Rawalpindi, Val's family had hired a cook-bearer and a houseboy for me. I drove to Pindi Palace where everything had been done for me and moved my items to my new home, which was yucky and in a village of Muslims who hated America but loved our aid money. It was a bit spooky being the only foreigner in the area, but, as I have said, I was never afraid because God was

Pakistan – 1963-1964

with me. My cook was very good and cooked curry as I had requested. The house was not very comfortable, but at least I could get a little rest since I moved away from the base and the natives didn't know where I moved to. It was very cold with just two space heaters. I used one of the heaters to warm the bathroom up above freezing ± 10 degrees and also heat the water to something a few degrees below the room temperature. A water pipe came out of the floor four inches from the wall and went to a somewhat shower head near the ceiling. Assuming the well pump had power and was working and the well had water in it, all I had to do was open the valve, and water would gush out onto the floor. (You guessed right: no tub or curtains.) Using my much-doubted scientific brain, I put my little kerosene heater on the floor directly under the shower nozzle thirty minutes before stripping and stepping directly under the shower head. I would then open the valve just enough to wet my body and give me third-degree burns. The next step was to soap my body and turn the water on to wash the soap off. Well before half of the soap was off, the fourteen ounces of hot/warm water had disappeared, and I was freezing again. Oh, the joys of living in Pakistan. After that first night of insanity, I drove out to base for a little humor listening to the avionics technicians crying about me being away from home so much.

When I got home expecting my cook bearer to have a big pot of spicy chicken vindaloo curry ready for dinner, I found him and my houseboy getting acquainted with about thirty poor villagers. I had a single outdoor water faucet inside the fence which was the only source of water for the village. Everyone came there daily for buckets of water. All of the people were cheering and shouting, and I was told that they were thanking me.

One Friday, the one-eyed colonel invited all of the reps to a party at the officers' club the next night. They didn't have curry either, so I wondered why I went. All of the officers seemed angry, so I had to ask why. It was because the US had sent a four-hundred-million-dollar aid package to them and was insisting that they use it to help the public, but they wanted the money to kick the rear end of India. I had a logical solution: tell the USA to keep the money and keep peace with India. They thought I was insane to suggest anything like that. (Breaking news: On Sunday morning, 9-29-24, the guest speaker at Blessed Hope Baptist Church, Hudson, FL, was Indian Pastor K. Vijayanandam Kammaraguntar. His home is in Hyderabad, Telangana, S. India, and he was on a five-day speaking tour to raise funds for his ministry of "Planting Churches". He has already started two to four hundred Baptist Churches in India. He and I had a long discussion about my time in India/Pakistan and how my favorite food was Indian curry. He came to our home in Hudson and taught Edith how to cook curry. A few days later, we took him to the Outback Steakhouse for a large steak. He and his family and numerous other Indian friends are on my Facebook page.)

Valerie wanted us to go to the Mangla Dam Project and spend the weekend with some of her friends. I wasn't sure that I wanted to do that, but agreed. The "Project" was to build a huge earth-filled dam and hydroelectric generating system that would supply power for housing areas. They had a multitude of bulldozers, cranes, trucks, and other earth-

Pakistan – 1963-1964

moving equipment. The company heading up the program had built a small city in this wilderness, including a grocery store, supermarket, streets, houses, condos, tennis courts, bowling lanes, swimming pool, etc.. This was a gated community; only residents and invited guests could enter. Someone was digging deep into our funds. The family that invited us for the weekend was the father, mother, and daughter that had come to Pindi Palace for dinner. All of them gave us a big hug and introduced me to neighbors and friends. Valerie knew all of them; she seemed to have a lot of friends. We had a good time, and I was already dreading the thought of going back to work the next day. Rawalpindi is at the foothill of the Himalayan Mountain chain. Valerie and her five siblings were educated by nuns at a Catholic Convent in the mountains north of Rawalpindi. It was too cold and dreary for the priests and pope to even visit. I couldn't help wondering why Cliff would send the kids to a dump like that with little or no heat and extremely cold weather when there was a well-equipped Catholic school near their house in Rawalpindi.

Not too long after that weekend trip, the Brady Bunch started loading all kinds of things on the roof rack of their small Leland Mini. All of them were small in stature, so they got inside and set off for England. That was not a pleasant trip in first-class seats of a jet airliner. They had to drive north to Peshawar, turn left and drive through the Khyber Pass into Afghanistan, work down into Iran, turn right through several countries, load onto a ferry that crosses the English Channel, and drive to your destination. They would camp out all of the way. This was suicidal. The war that Pakistan had started was in motion when I boarded a plane back to Atlanta, Georgia.

Chapter 7
Azores Islands, Scotland, Spain & Libya - 1964-1967

After a few weeks back home with Ricky and my parents, I spent about four weeks in the home office. My next assignment was to be covering the Pacific fleet of C-130 Rescue & Recovery Aircraft. The Lockheed Training Department instructors were teaching classes on the Fulton Recovery System, a system that would allow a C-130 aircraft to pick up two men from a dense jungle without landing. I was scheduled to attend the class, so I made the short walk and sat down in the classroom. The other students were from the USAF Rescue & Recovery Units in the Pacific that I would be covering, so I wanted to use this opportunity to get acquainted with them. The instructor issued training manuals to each of us and began teaching. When we broke for lunch, I went to one of the Lockheed dining rooms with the other students. After lunch, we were seated in the classroom and started getting edgy because the instructor had not returned; then the training manager informed us that the instructor was ill. The students were dismissed and told to be back the next morning at eight, but he asked me to stay. He told me that the instructor was very sick and asked me to teach the course. Mama, come get me and take me back to the farm! I said, "Why me? You have several instructors, so hand the pointer to one of them". He replied that they didn't know the system. Big deal, neither do I, but I agreed to do it. I took the manuals home and studied them for three hours. Very much easier than avionics and other systems that I had been teaching, so this would be a snap and would be helpful in the future. About six days later, the students thanked me and looked forward to working with me in the Pacific Area.

One of the C-130H Rescue & Recovery aircraft was to undergo cold weather testing at a hangar near Fort Walton Beach, FL. Every series of C-130 aircraft with new systems had to go through a series of tests before they could be delivered. (That is one aircraft of the series.) I had to suffer another vacation with pay. Woe am I. Must have had a good instinct when I got home from Pakistan and bought a new red British Sprite Convertible. The bad thing was the top had to be lowered and raised manually, so you had to move off the highway quickly to pull it up and latch it to the windshield. By then, the car was full of water, and the car was not equipped with air conditioning. I don't understand why anyone in the coastal areas of Florida would buy a convertible because they are always out of step with the popup showers. The aircraft was moved into a hangar that can take temperatures down to minus thirty degrees Fahrenheit and up to plus one hundred thirty degrees (I might be off slightly). This was similar to my arctic survival in Colorado at minus thirty degrees and to the days I played golf in Pakistan with one hundred seventeen. The joy of living at Fort Walton Beach was quenched, but Lockheed was always on hand to cheer me up.

I received a frantic call. The rep who was to cover the Atlantic area had what was believed to be a heart attack shortly after he arrived on Lajes USAF Base, Portugal. He was coming back to the USA for treatment and would brief me before I left to replace him, so the home office was

Azores Islands, Scotland, Spain & Libya – 1964-1967

making my airline reservations already. Whoa, someone is out of step, I am getting ready for a trip in the opposite direction, and I would rather stay near Rick instead of another overseas tour. I heard a click proving that no one listens to me. I drove back to Marietta where I tried to convince Ricky and myself that I had to leave again, but even I couldn't understand why. Only God knew, and He had not told me.

The next morning, I saw the man who supposedly had a heart attack, and I knew why he was back. I had seen him numerous times when I was working as a flight line electrician, and he was in supply. When we needed a new component, our supervisor would take a form with the part number on it to a tiny wire cage and give it to this man who would go into a warehouse and give the form to another person who would "pull the part". This man would take it to our supervisor. I don't think the supply rep was allowed to go near the aircraft, so I was curious about why he got a job that he wasn't qualified for. I took him into a room and demanded that he explain. He asked me not to say anything; he promised that he would ask for his hourly job in supply because his heart condition would make it prohibitive for him to travel. I said, "Do it. Let me know if I can help you". He did call me a few years later and gave him a supply job in Iran. I was told that grown men don't cry, but that is not true. I have cried a lot about my family over the years. The people who are ashamed to cry must not love their families as much as I do.

That happened the next day when I left Ricky and flew first class on Pan American Airways to Santa Maria Island,

Azores, Portugal. I had to ride a puddle jumper to the USAF base on Lajes, Azores, Portugal. Another déjà vu. I was there in 1954 and again in 1955 while in the USAF. A bus picked me up and took me to the control tower where I met the base commander. He confirmed that I was Bill Walls from Lockheed and then told me that a USAF C-130 had taken off in Saudi Arabia, and one of the tires exploded during takeoff. That's all that they knew, but the aircraft had to land here. I was seated in a flight operations seat with a headset on and the base commander's orders that it was in my hands. Mama, come get me. Several fire trucks and ambulances were already lined up on the side of the runway, and warning horns were warning everyone not to start sightseeing. I asked the pilot what his ETA was, how much longer his fuel would last, and what he knew about the condition of the landing gear. He said he would arrive in fifteen minutes and had about enough fuel for fifty minutes, but he knew very little about the landing gear condition. I told the pilot to make a low approach with the landing gear extended and fly two hundred feet above the control tower and two hundred feet east of the tower so I could assess the situation. He replied, "Roger, Will Do". I saw that this was a cool and knowledgeable pilot. The commander had a phone in his hand, and I asked if he was in touch with the fire trucks. He replied in the affirmative, so I told him to tell the firemen to stand by to lay a solid sheet of foam down the runway when you give the orders. The C-130 made a slow flyby, and I had an excellent view to see that the right front main landing gear tire explosion had destroyed the door and metal structure in the area. All else was OK. I relayed this to the pilot and told him to go around one time and land on the runway; do not

Azores Islands, Scotland, Spain & Libya – 1964-1967

use your brakes, use only the propellers for braking. "We are going to lay foam on the runway to prevent sparks. Everything is going to be OK". The commander told the firemen to foam the runway and stand by off the runway during landing. I started praying, asking God to help us, and laid it in His hands. The aircraft made a perfect landing and turned off onto a taxiway where the engines were shut down. Meanwhile, the firemen were spraying foam into the wheel wells just in case the tires and brakes had overheated. I knew the pilot had only used propellers for braking, so this was a double precaution. USAF standard protocol. The commander took me up to the BOQ (Bachelor Officer Quarters) for check-in. He then said that he would like to give me a commendation, but I was only doing my duty, so he should give the pilot and flight crew a commendation. I believe that only God is worthy. This housing is always noisy, so I spent most of the night thinking about home.

The Azores are a small group of islands in the North Atlantic that belong to Portugal. They are volcanic and very rocky. Lajes Air Base is the home of the USAF 65th Air Wing and a squadron of Air Rescue & Recovery C-130H aircraft. It is a very strategic location for traffic in the Atlantic Ocean. The airfield is in the valley, and the living area is up a steep hill. The whole island is volcanic rock. The officers' club is open twenty-four/seven. There is a rod & gun club, PX, Commissary, whiskey store, bowling lanes, school, dormitory for teachers, etc., on top of this "hill". The USAF also has a nice golf course about six miles up another hill. It is hard to imagine where they found enough soil to cover the rock, but I soon learned that they did not purchase enough.

If you do not make a shallow swing at the golf ball, your iron club tries to create images in the stone. Not recommended!

The squadron commander who welcomed me aboard was a tall colonel. He asked about my favorite sports, and I replied that basketball was my favorite in high school, but I had not played in the last fourteen years, so my favorite now is golf. He said, "Our squadron needs you on both teams. Basketball is on Friday night, and the golf league plays on Saturdays. Thank you for helping us. What C-130H systems do you teach?" I said, "Name it, and I'll teach it". He was very pleased and introduced me to the training sergeant. Lockheed Georgia had fourteen copies of each training manual and appropriate films placed on the airline flight that my predecessor was on, so I knew they were in place here. The sergeant introduced me to the Allison Rep and the Hamilton Standard Rep that would be traveling with me. Everyone asked how the rep that I replaced was doing. I replied that he did not have a heart attack and was OK. Several people needed to learn the Fulton Recovery System and then other parts of the aircraft, so the six weeks went quickly. Then one of the C-130H aircraft flew the other two reps and me to Prestwick, Scotland, where another squadron of the C-130H aircraft was based. The crew at Prestwick unloaded our training data and took it to the training center. I managed to rent a car, and we went into town to check out some apartments and houses for rent. I decided on a four-bedroom house on the beach in Ayr, Scotland, and they wanted to share a two-bedroom apartment. I dropped them off with their bags and drove to my house on the beach that was near Ayr Golf Course, which is on the PGA tour. Some years the Scottish Open is played there, and the British Open

Azores Islands, Scotland, Spain & Libya – 1964-1967

is occasionally held there. That should be suitable for now. They have two seasons per year: cold and colder, with some rain expected every day. During the longest days of the year, you can tee off at nine PM and play eighteen holes of golf. It is twilight from about one AM until daylight at around three AM when it becomes bright very rapidly. The opposite is true in the winter.

I went to the base at eight the next morning and arranged a series of classes for six weeks. It was like a breath of fresh air working with the US Air Force instead of the Pakistan Air Force. I was supposed to cover three locations, but the third base would not receive their aircraft until six months later. At some time, I wrote a letter to Valerie to see if she and her family were having trouble in Pakistan. I also told her about my roving assignment. She replied that everything had settled down, but she would fly to London and stay with her aunt in Harlow on the north side of London so we could get together occasionally. I was scheduled to be in Scotland until January, so I went down and got a motel in Harlow one weekend. Her aunt invited me for dinner one night, so I met her and her children, and saw Valerie. It was nice to meet them. It never ceased to amaze me to see people whose ancestors moved from Europe ages ago and married natives in India or another country to the point none of them had citizenship unless the country granted them citizenship. No one has asked me to get involved, so I will get back to my memoirs. So many problems I have to leave for others to solve!

About mid-January 1965, one of the Prestwick C-130 aircraft was used to take the other two reps and me back to the Azores for six more weeks of teaching, playing golf, and bowling. I quit the squadron basketball team because I was having to play too much. I couldn't understand why the other men even played the game. I am sure the guys were good at some sports, but basketball was not their forte. In March, we were back in Scotland for six weeks. Valerie came up for a visit, and we flew over to Northern Ireland for a long weekend. Belfast is the capital of the north, and Dublin is the capital of the south. North Ireland is still part of Great Britain, but some citizens wanted to be freed to unite with the south. After several years of civil war in the late twentieth century, citizens of Belfast voted to remain part of the British Empire. Ireland is an Island country. Great Britain (England, Scotland & Wales) is also an Island. (Take a look at a world map if you aren't familiar with that trivia.) The whole area is breathtakingly beautiful. It seemed like a few hours, and I was back in Scotland.

I called Scottish Aviation, a company at Prestwick that is authorized to build a few structural items for C-130 aircraft, identified myself, and asked to speak with the general manager. He was on the phone immediately. He knew my name and that I would be in the area occasionally, so he asked whether I could go over to see him. I agreed and drove over to the facility. He and the deputy director showed me around the impressive facility. They insisted that I have lunch with them, which I reluctantly did. The only delicious food in Great Britain is found in Indian restaurants, but the food that day wasn't bad. They wanted to know whether I played golf, a necessary question where golf originated, so I replied in the affirmative, but that I was only an average golfer. They were sure I was only being modest; not so. The

Azores Islands, Scotland, Spain & Libya – 1964-1967

general manager had a well-underrated four handicap, his deputy had a six (a person never becomes a deputy if his handicap is too close to the manager's), and mine was fourteen. They were members of Old Troon Course, one of the oldest courses in the world, and they could take me as their guest. I quickly advised that I did not play when it was raining (if it isn't raining, it's only a short time away in Scotland and either cold or colder). I was ordered to put a warm coat and raincoat on and be at the course at ten next Saturday. It was raining when I left home and continued through the day. Of course, we had to carry our clubs, so I was drenched, cold, and not so happy by the time we finished the round. The manager and his deputy had scores in the mid-70s, and mine was 98. Even though I was freezing, we shook hands and agreed that we probably wouldn't play together again. Golf originated in a cow pasture in Scotland, and the courses look very much like the one on our farm in South Georgia, with the exception of the rain and cold weather. St. Andrews is the oldest course, and it is next to impossible to get a ticket to play there. I refused an all-expense paid trip to play there several years later. Val stayed for a few days more and then went back to Harlow.

Sometime around the end of April, I was in the Azores. While going through the same motions of teaching and also playing golf, I was told that the squadron in Scotland had relocated to Seville, Spain; therefore, Scotland would no longer be on my tour. At the end of six weeks, one C-130H aircraft took the other two reps and me to the USAF base near Seville, Spain. Close is a misnomer; it is sixty miles from the front gate of the base to Seville, so I rented a car and drove into the city where I rented a hotel room. The other two guys stayed at the officers' quarters on base. Due to ignorance, they didn't want to eat "foreign food". I counted this as my blessing. Inflation had not gotten into Spain at that time, so I had a very nice room in the second-best hotel in the city for less than three dollars per night. The drawback was I had to eat delicious "foreign food". I got up early the next morning and drove sixty-five miles to the air base and started looking for the office. I was walking down the hallway, and my attention suddenly turned to a room full of enlisted men. The chief master sergeant and I immediately knew one another, so we shook hands, hugged, and shook hands; then he explained to all of his troops that we had gone through arctic survival and ParaRescue training together, but I chickened out and left before the parachute training finished. I was called Willie Walls in the air force, and his name is Willie Williams. His team had to know the whole story because this was just too ironic. I briefly told what I had done after leaving that training, and Willie filled in after that. He was then in charge of all jumpers in the Atlantic area, so we continued to see each other during my tour. It was great to renew an old friendship, but we never communicated after my assignment ended the next year. It's sad but true that most military friendships end that way.

Seville is in the southern area of Spain, and Madrid, the capital, is in the north central. There are numerous tourist resorts all over the country, and the primary income is tourism. A US Navy Base at Rota, Spain, is about sixty miles east of the USAF Base. A squadron of Lockheed P-3 Orion Maritime Patrol aircraft was based there, so it was my duty to drive over occasionally to see if there was any assistance needed. The Isle of Gibraltar is south of Seville on the Strait

Azores Islands, Scotland, Spain & Libya – 1964-1967

of Gibraltar. This is a narrow waterway that separates Gibraltar from Morocco. In 1966, Gibraltar was owned by Great Britain, so a fence separated it from Spain. We drove down and parked in a lot, then paid a fee to Spain in order to walk through a gate. After that, we walked across "No Man's Land" to another gate that was guarded by the British Army where there was no payment due. The Rock of Gibraltar is another tourist attraction, so Spain resented that the British Empire had given it to Great Britain. To rub salt into the wound, the British had huge floodlights shining on the rock all night.

About this time, I received a call from Wheelus USAF base in Tripoli, Libya, advising me that they had received their C-130H aircraft and had declared an emergency for me. This gave me top priority on any flight from Spain to Libya. I quickly packed a bag, and one of the C-130H aircraft flew me to Kaiserslautern AB in Germany. As soon as we parked on the ramp, someone grabbed my bag and ushered me into a staff car. We went up to a USAF T-39 Sabreliner business jet where my driver notified the pilot that I had top priority for the flight. The base commander had just boarded and had to deplane. He was an unhappy camper and came up very close and demanded that I explain how a civilian in a business suit could get priority over a colonel. I gave him a big smile and told him to take it up with his boss as I brushed him aside and took his seat. I guess he was still cursing when the jet engines drowned him out. The other four passengers were silent all the way, probably thinking that I had to be CIA. I didn't offer any information. I don't remember what the big emergency was, but it must not have taken very long to resolve it. It was almost time to rotate down here, so the officials in Spain loaded the rest of my clothing and data on one of their C-130H aircraft when it brought the Allison and Hamilton Standard reps to Tripoli.

Libya is located on the northeast side of the African continent, and King Idris was the monarch in Libya when I was there in 1966 and 1967. I saw Libyan Army Lt. Col. Muammar Gaddafi at air force headquarters on this visit. His army and the Libyan air force headquarters were in the same building as the USAF. I was in a meeting with someone when Gaddafi opened the door and started shouting. One of the US officers chased him out and told me that Gaddafi was a troublemaker who was up to no good. The Libyan air force had about ten antique aircraft, and the army had less equipment, so all they could do was stir up trouble. The king was a moderate, and Gaddafi was a radical Islamist. The king had allowed luxury hotels, casinos, and a lot of other things to be built in Tripoli. I lived in a hotel and drove back and forth in a rental car to work. There was a golf course, but I only played it once because it is on the edge of the desert. It is simply a sand trap from the tee through the oil-soaked browns (aka greens). Not worth a second round.

I was back in Libya for the usual three-month visit a year later when Egypt, Syria, and Jordan attacked Israel, thus starting The Six-Day War. Six days is how long it took the Arabs to retreat when Israel began a counter-offensive. The Israeli air force could have destroyed all of the tanks and ground troops in the desert but only wiped out a few to speed them up. The Libyans came and flew their pitiful aircraft across town to the airport to show their contempt for the USA's support of Israel. I had moved to the base to provide

Azores Islands, Scotland, Spain & Libya – 1964-1967

close support for the C-130s that were being used for evacuation of all American citizens in the country. When that was completed, I was transported to the Azores for another six weeks. The rotations continued as scheduled, and I was back in Spain in August and September 1967. The temperature was over one hundred twenty in Seville, and I saw in the paper that the highest temperature that had ever been recorded was one hundred eighty-seven in the Iranian desert the day before. I said that I would never go there, but had to eat my words later that year when I was assigned to go there.

Valerie and I decided that it was time to either get married or call it quits. It was difficult because of our differences and an on-again, off-again relationship, but we decided to tolerate each other. I gave her an engagement ring, and she hopped on a plane to Pakistan to break the news to her family. She would have a wedding dress made in Rawalpindi and meet me back in Spain four weeks later. My next and final stop was Libya toward the end of September. I got back to work as soon as possible because I knew that there were only four weeks left on the contract with the USAF. I saw Gaddafi at headquarters and hoped that someone would find a way to control him, but found later that he and a few officers revolted against King Idris when he was out of the country, and he took control of Libya in 1969. My contract expired a week earlier than expected, and Lockheed told me to come straight back to the home office, so I called Valerie to give the good/bad news to her. (I went back to Tripoli about 1975 when I was Program Manager in Iran. We had a small team in Libya because the US Government had allowed Gaddafi to purchase C-130 aircraft. Go figure that!

You might recall the time later when Gaddafi attacked US military sites, and President Reagan sent fighter/bombers from Europe one night to strike Gaddafi's home and military sites, thus putting the fear of God into him. He was no longer of use to radicals, so he was assassinated in 2011. Hillary Clinton botched the attack on the US Consulate in Benghazi, Libya, two years later, causing four US patriots to be killed. The US Senate caused her to resign as Secretary of State.)

Chapter 8
LOCKHEED EMPLOYMENT - Iran: 1967-1977

Upon return, I was told that Lockheed Georgia had received a contract to set up a C-130 aircraft overhaul program in Tehran, Iran. Usually, Lockheed Aircraft Service handles that type of program, but Iran insisted that our division run it. Six Service reps would do planning and preparation and advise a team of Iranians regarding how to do the work. I had to ask a few simple questions: "Do you really believe that this is possible, and why are you telling me?" The reply was: "Several people say that it cannot be done, and we want you to prove them wrong. Will you do it?" I was upset that I was being used; no one had ever had to spend this much continual time overseas without time in the home office. I was ready to walk out the door. Someone finally got me to settle down enough to ask me what they could do to change my mind. I said: "First of all, I am going to spend some time with my son and parents, then I want first-class airline tickets, hotels, and ground transportation anywhere I go in the future, and I want it in writing!". That was agreed, and all of this was ready when I walked back in after my vacation with Ricky and my parents. I still thought that I should have resigned from my job instead of giving an ultimatum. It was too late now, though.

Bill D, the man who was our team leader, met me at the airport and took me to the best hotel in Tehran. We had a long talk, and we immediately clicked. This appeared to be a knowledgeable, no-nonsense man. This gave me confidence that we would make the program work. I told him that my fiancé was supposed to be there the next week, so I wanted to get a reservation for her and find a house that I could have ready when we got married shortly thereafter. With his help, it was accomplished. I found a man who immediately moved furniture into a newly built apartment that I rented. An American pastor of a non-titled church made arrangements for our marriage two days after Valerie arrived; I loaded the apartment with food, and bought a new yellow Pekan sedan (British automobile), and was hard at work when Valerie arrived. She was a bit upset that we were going to be married before her parents could come, but I tried to comfort her by telling her that I could claim her as a dependent to reduce my income tax. Guess there was nothing I could do to make her happy, because she even hated the beautiful yellow sedan that I bought. She claimed that it was a putrid color. The marriage was going to be as rocky as our three years of on-again, off-again dating had proven.

I went out to the C-130 aircraft hangar that had just been built for the C-130 overhaul program. It was just off the runway at Iranian Air Force Headquarters on the outskirts of Tehran. One of the two C-130 Bases is at Mehrabad International Airport on the opposite side of Tehran, and the other C-130 base is at Shiraz in the southern part of Iran. The Alborz Mountain Range is a short distance from the airport. When an aircraft takes off from the airport or the air base, the pilot must begin a ninety-degree left turn ASAP, otherwise the infamous sudden death syndrome wipes out everyone on board. This did happen a few years later.

LOCKHEED EMPLOYMENT – Iran: 1967-1977

Iran is very wealthy in oil, natural gas, and many other things. It was formerly the Persian Empire; but has been through a series of wars over the ages. In an attempt to stabilize the country, the CIA reportedly used power to put the Shah in power after World War 2. He was the leader of the Sunni sect, which is only ten percent of Iran's population, and the Sunnis are the most moderate of Islam. The Shi'ite sect comprises eighty-eight percent of the population in Iran, and they are very radical. The Shah was the best ally the USA and Israel had in the world. Jimmy Carter double-crossed him when he became president. We will forever pay for that stupid or perhaps intentional blunder.

Bill introduced me to Mechanical Engineer Paddy Henderson; Electronics Specialist John D; Propeller Specialist Fred H; and another man who supposedly knew hydraulic systems. I knew John very well but knew absolutely nothing about the others. It was disclosed that Tom Cleland, Director of Product Support at Lockheed Georgia, and Bill had started their careers with Lockheed in 1939 when the company had a contract to repair aircraft in Belfast, North Ireland. Bill was a mechanic, and Tom was an electronics specialist. Bill married Ann, an Irish girl, then Bill and Tom became friends with Paddy and Patty Henderson. After World War 2, Bill, Paddy, and Tom continued their careers at Lockheed California in Burbank. Tom worked his way up through the ranks and moved to Lockheed Georgia when they leased the plant from the US Government. Sometime later, he was promoted to Director of Product Support. When the contract was received to set up the C-130 overhaul facility, he directed that Bill and Paddy be members of the team. Bill was an excellent choice, but Paddy simply was his friend, so I had to live with it. I don't believe Paddy had attended college, so it was questionable how he became a mechanical engineer, but it was not up to me to question that either. I knew that Bill and I had a very difficult job ahead.

Valerie didn't want to see our apartment until we were married, but I checked her out of the hotel and dropped the baggage off on the way to the church. All of the team was invited to the wedding and to dinner afterwards. John agreed to be best man and his wife, Linda, to be bridesmaid. I did have corsages for everyone, so we sailed through the wedding, the dinner, and the drive home. The trouble started when I picked her up to cross the threshold and suggested that she was gaining weight. It got worse when she asked where we were going on honeymoon, and I told her that we would spend the weekend getting her into the cooking and cleaning mode, then I had to get to work on Monday while she got into her job. Maybe we will take our kids with us on a honeymoon in a few years. She was not a happy camper, thus we both realized that we should not have started dating three years earlier. We agreed that we now must do our best to make it work.

I stayed busy nine hours a day trying to be sure all of the one hundred plus Iranian men on the program were capable of working their jobs, but when the first aircraft arrived, I soon found that they were not capable. They were smart, but few of them had been completely trained. We had allocated ten weeks to remove and replace time-change components and thoroughly inspect everything else. This would include washing the outside of the aircraft, cleaning the inside of all areas, and finally having a test flight. Four weeks into the first aircraft, another one would arrive, so we would have up to three aircraft at a time in various stages of the inspection. It got very involved, and I was trying to give hands-on assistance to people from all of the shops. The crews refused to do flight tests unless I was onboard to instruct them on each step. This meant that I had to be in too many places at the same time, and this put a strain on my home life too. Meanwhile, Valerie had started having lunch with Linda and a few other ladies, and they started bowling too. I had new bowling balls drilled for us so that we could go bowling together on weekends. At some point, we were introduced to Les and Mary Jayasinghe. He was from Sri Lanka, and she was from a small island south of New Zealand, and they had three kids. Les was a mechanic for Iran Air, and Mary was a homemaker. They had friends from several countries, so we intermingled and became good friends. Several months later, we bowled in a league with them.

Dropping back to the present time, Valerie had prepared my favorite food: Indian curry. She was smiling and dreamy, so I asked what had happened. She told me to eat, and we could talk later. After dinner, we sat on the couch, and she said that she was pregnant, "Are you as happy as I am?". I guessed so but had to ask what happened. I knew that was not the proper way to phrase my words, but she was so perturbed by my question that she explained about the birds and bees. I had heard the big boys talking, but when she explained it, all I could say was: "Now I see". It was not the time for my sense of humor!

Bill and I worked together to prepare a list of components that would be required for each C-130 before it was scheduled to be there. The air force had a good inventory, but some items would have to be purchased from Lockheed. Whoever planned for this program had no knowledge about actual requirements. A supply rep would have been a blessing. We took the list to Lt. General Toufanian, Director of Logistics, and he always signed an order that we sent via air mail to our home office. All of the jobs allowed me an opportunity to spread the word of Jesus Christ to many people who would not have heard the word otherwise. No glory for me; it is all about HIM. This happened in every country, but I did not realize it at the time that God was using me to reach out to people that others couldn't reach. I missed some opportunities and frequently wanted to quit my job, but HE gently chastised me and guided me. On July 20, 1968, God gave me another wonderful son, William Jeffry Walls. I thanked my Lord for HIS blessings of two wonderful sons. Could it possibly get any better?

When the anesthetics started wearing off, Valerie asked if it was a boy or girl. I said, "Boy". "Is he handsome?" "Very". "Is he healthy?" "Very". "Does he have five fingers and toes?" "Six," but I quickly said that I was only joking when tears began. I was again informed that I have a weird sense of humor. I was totally ignored when a nurse laid Jeff on her shoulder. About the only time I was allowed to touch Jeff was when he needed to be changed or cried for a bottle of milk in the middle of the night. I could not get her attention by accidentally rolling over into her, so I had no choice other than getting up.

LOCKHEED EMPLOYMENT – Iran: 1967-1977

The Iranian officials were so pleased with our work that someone in the home office decided to send someone over to get the credit. He was to be the regional representative, and Bill was promoted to resident representative. Bill should have been promoted, and the other guy should have stayed on his position as plumber's helper. Instead, he set up an office at home and waited for someone to tell him what to brag about to the home office. Our best source of semi-rapid communications was by telex, so someone had to go downtown to the International Hotel to send or pick up messages. This should have been the responsibility of the new regional rep, but he stayed busy at home, so Bill D. often had to find time to do this.

Colonel Nezam Hagagot was the officer in charge of the overhaul program. His office was next door to ours, so we came to know him very well. Bill and Paddy and their wives became close friends with Nezam and his wife. General Toufanian came to the hangar at least once a week to check on the program. He ignored everyone until he found me, then he held my hand, and we walked throughout the area as I brought him up to date. If he discovered that some people weren't working, he asked me why. It was my responsibility to keep them on the job, disregarding Nezam and everyone else. When the weather was very hot or cold, it was difficult to keep everyone on the job, so I explained it to the general, and huge air conditioning units were installed. General Toufanian told me that I no longer needed an appointment to see anyone at headquarters, just walk through their side door, and I could have attention immediately. He assured me that no one would waste my time. I thanked him, and he disappeared in his staff car without saying goodbye to anyone else. The same procedure occurred every week, and the Shah came down from his palace with a small army to see what was being accomplished. All of the Iranian workers and the Lockheed representatives lined up side by side about fifty feet across from the Shah. Everyone stood at attention, and somehow I was directed to step forward. That put me farther ahead of everyone else, and I was already in front of the Shah. General Toufanian was standing beside Him, then saluted and introduced all of the reps. When I was introduced, I did not bow but gave a smart salute, and the Shah nodded. I do not bow to anyone except Jesus Christ. I don't know why I received special recognition, but frankly believed that I deserved it if anyone did. When the regional rep was informed, he was livid because he had not been involved; I smirked at him, which made him angrier. I was the only happy person in sight.

My father had developed diabetes and started sneaking around and eating fresh fruit off the trees. His diabetes got out of control; gangrene developed in one leg, causing the doctor to amputate it, but the gangrene killed my father very quickly. Someone in my family called my home office and asked that I be notified so that I could get home in time for the funeral. The regional rep called me late one afternoon and asked me to drive up to his house because we needed to discuss something, so I did. He fumbled with some papers, then told me that my father had died. I went back to the house to discuss this with Valerie. She insisted that I go immediately because it would take too long to arrange the trip. I called the airport to make reservations and then called Bill D and asked him to notify Lockheed that I was on the way. My nephew had Ricky in the car when they picked me

LOCKHEED EMPLOYMENT – Iran: 1967-1977

up at the Atlanta airport. Ricky and I were SO happy to be together again. A group of my siblings, plus nephews and nieces, were with my mother. Everyone wanted to know why I had not come sooner, but I sat down beside my mother and wrapped my arms around her. She couldn't hold it any longer, just started crying and saying, "I knew you would be here if someone would just...". My siblings and their families left the next day, giving me more time with Ricky and my mother. I knew that I had to go back to Iran but wanted to make them as comfortable as possible before I left. At the last moment, I went back to Marietta so that Ricky could return to school and I could have some hard discussions with Lockheed officials about the goof-up regarding notification of my father's death. It only took a few minutes to lay the blame on the regional rep and put things in motion to recall him.

I got back into all of my work duties and spent time with my family. We took Jeff when we went bowling and every other place. He was very content in a pram because everyone insisted on cuddling him and showing him to everyone in sight. It was hard on us because we had to keep our eyes on those activities. We spent more time with Les and Mary Jayasinghe; we took them out for dinner in Tehran and at our house, and they invited us to their house too. One night, Les introduced me to English darts. At first glance, it looks like a game for sissies, but there is a lot of precision and planning involved. He tore me up for the first three games, but it was a fight to the finish the fourth, and I easily won the fifth. He decided not to play anymore. I bought a dartboard, darts, and other paraphernalia the next day, then Val and I played together every moment for the week. Les never came close to beating me again. He played in the international darts league, and I was asked to join the team. This was the favorite sport in Iran with thousands of teams throughout the country and well over a hundred teams in Tehran. British Airways and the Kayhan Newspaper sponsored the sport. The newspaper published weekly standings until the top 10 teams, doubles, and individuals met for the finals that were held in an enormous auditorium in Tehran. Every seat and standing place were filled, and no movement or whispers were allowed when a person was set up to throw a dart. It was breathtaking. Our team had one man from Sri Lanka, one from the USA, two from the Philippines, two from Australia, and one from India. All of them except me worked for Iran Airlines. We bowled on Wednesday nights, and I played darts Friday nights while Val kept Jeff. About twenty people followed our team in the beginning and doubled when we started a winning streak. Our home base was in a large room of a downtown hotel, and other teams had similar venues. We would play a home game and an away game back and forth through the season until the playoffs. We became one of the top ten teams, which put us in the playoffs, but we never won the team championship. I won two consecutive Iranian individual championship titles with huge trophies. I selected Valerie for my partner when we decided to play the mixed doubles the second year, and we came in second place, even though she had never played in the league or even watched any game. I choked with a dart that would have given us first place. I had never missed a shot like that. Regardless, I never played another competitive game after that because my work load did not permit the time.

LOCKHEED EMPLOYMENT – Iran: 1967-1977

In 1970, we took Jeff on our honeymoon to Epping, England, thus fulfilling my promise when we married. Valerie's mother, father, and two brothers had moved there from Pakistan. I had arranged for Ricky to meet us there to help the brothers spend time together and see sights in England and Scotland. This made me very happy at the same time. Rick was more reserved, a planner, and Jeff was on the move and chattering from the beginning. After a few days in the back seat cruising through the two countries, Rick finally had to ask, "Doesn't he ever shut up?". Perhaps someday, but not in the near future, though! That was a bright spot, although all of us enjoyed the scenery. It always ended too soon, though!

In 1971, the C-130 aircraft overhaul program became the beginning of Iran Aircraft Industries. Lockheed Aircraft Services hired a huge number of bodies to do the job six of us had done, and not as effectively. My weird sense of humor caused me to smile. I washed my hands of it and moved on. Bill D retired, and the regional rep's position was still open, so Lockheed Georgia Vice President Dave Crockett canceled those slots and created the position of Program Manager, reporting to him. That was my new job, going from salary grade six to twelve; unheard of. This happened because all of the top generals praised me for my hard work. I immediately praised the Lord for his blessings on me. I always tried to be worthy of my pay and appreciated having a job. I had to get back on it. I moved into a large office in Tehran and had a full-time secretary. I still had eighty Lockheed employees and their families to oversee and other duties also. The payment records for everyone who worked for me were handled by a CPA firm in Geneva, Switzerland, so I had to make occasional trips there and on to London, England.

One day when I was packing my bag to make the trip, I made a terrible mistake by asking Valerie if I could pick up something for her. I expected her to ask for a diamond mounted in a gold piece of jewelry or something like that, but she asked for "a large selection of smelly Swiss cheese!". That was unthinkable, but she repeated it "Twice". When I told the director of the CPA office what I wanted, he and his staff giggled in French/German, and that was exceptionally wicked. He insisted on taking me to the best store that sold nothing but cheese. The sales people were fluent in English but not in South Georgia Redneck, so he interpreted for me. The salesman asked me if I wanted a half kilo of his favorite smelly cheese, and I told him that I would like a kilo of every type in the store. All of the sales personnel gathered around and asked me to repeat it. I handed my new leather carry-on bag to him, and he filled it and quickly zipped it. Swiss Air checked me in without looking at my carry-on, and customs and security at Heathrow Airport didn't look at me. I spent a week in London, and the weather was hot. When I was getting ready to board the British Air flight to Tehran, the security agent told me to put my famous bag on the table for inspection. He unzipped the bag and made a very close inspection. He quickly zipped it and asked whether a bomb was in the bag. Without waiting for an answer, he gagged and passed out. Englishmen are very strange, and this is apparent when they gag on a smell and brag about their wives' cooking. I was picked up at the airport in Iran by my trusty chauffeur. He declined my offer of a kilo of Swiss cheese. He carried my bags in, and I led the way to advise

LOCKHEED EMPLOYMENT – Iran: 1967-1977

Val of my blessing for her, but she was busy, so I told the driver to put it in our number three fridge where it remained for over a year until our cook made a mistake and opened the bag. There were reports of chemical warfare, but I never disclosed the cheese that I purchased. Another fact weirder than the truth.

The Iranian workers, officers, and even the Shah were very pleased with what we had done for the country and gave all credit to me. They knew that I loved Iran, the people, and the government, so it was no secret to Lockheed or anyone except Valerie that I had been offered a job by the government; all I had to do was name the money and conditions. My heart was with my family and the USA, though, so I refused to accept it but later regretted it because I possibly would have been in a position to thwart Jimmy Carter's destruction of Iran.

A few months later, my good friend Jed Riding arrived in Iran with a contract for one hundred million dollars for thirty C-130 aircraft plus components and parts. He informed me that the C-130 production line would close in ten days unless we could get the Iranian government to purchase these aircraft. There was nothing in sight, so Lockheed would have to close the doors. I was about to lose my new job and everything, so this was not time to ask: "Why me, LORD?" We hopped into the company's new car, and my chauffeur took us to the Ministry of War. I boldly asked for an urgent meeting with the vice minister, so the receptionist told him of my request, and we were granted permission. I carefully explained the situation. He scanned through the contract and called the Shah. The vice minister told us that His Majesty agreed with the purchase; however, "I don't understand this wording". I took a quick look and told him that this was legalese, just lawyers attempting to confuse everyone, so we would change the wording. Jed said that we don't have time to send it to Burbank, and the contracts lawyers will not change it anyway, "so we are doomed". I told the minister that we would be back early the next morning. He said, "I know that you always find a way; I'll sign it when you come tomorrow". Jed was concerned that we would be fired for rewriting a contract. I told him that I would take the blame for changing it; regardless, we will not have a job if we don't take immediate action. My chauffeur drove us to my new home just outside the Shah's palace wall. The two of us went in for a delicious dinner with Val and Jeff. My office was on the outskirts of Tehran, which was twenty miles south of my home, but my secretary had left the office. I used an eraser to remove as much as possible of the offensive words, then used a manual typewriter to make the correction. Very crude bit of trash, but I knew it would fly. Jed kept saying that "we are dead!" I told him to keep the faith and sleep well. I thought it was funny because I wanted to quit many years ago anyway. Not many people appreciate my sense of humor. I took him to the hotel and said that we would pick him up at eight tomorrow. My driver took us to the ministry of war, and we were ushered into the vice minister's office. He signed the contract and told his secretary to make copies. While we were having a cup of tea, Jed had to ask, "Aren't you going to read the changes?". The minister replied that he knew it would be OK. Production of the C-130 is still continuing today: fifty years later.

LOCKHEED EMPLOYMENT – Iran: 1967-1977

One of the reps at Shiraz Air Base called and told me that his wife had terminal cancer and needed radiation treatments immediately. The only place to get a vial was in London, England. The problem was that it must be injected in less than twenty-four hours after mixing, or it would reach half-life and would be worthless. He provided all of the required information about the doctor, and I called my best friend, General Amir F, and he told me that he would take care of the problem. He returned my call about two hours later, "No Problem". The doctor in Shiraz would call a doctor in Tehran who would call an Iranian Doctor in London. He would mix the radioactive solution and put the vial in a safe container with dry ice, drive to Heathrow Airport, hand it to an Iran Air Pilot, who would bypass all checkpoints and make a scheduled five hour thirty minute direct flight to Tehran, hand it to a local pilot whose jet was next door, he would fly to Shiraz and hand it to the doctor who would inject the solution less than twelve hours after it was mixed. Piece of Cake. I didn't bother asking, "How?" but just said, "Thank you, My Friend". He replied, "My wife and I are looking forward to having you for lunch at our house tomorrow". Me too. We always prayed together, and he insisted on leading the prayers of thanks. I felt he would always be a solid Christian. He and his family were related to the Shah, and our friendship continued long after I left Iran. Amir had passed his Christian beliefs to numerous people that I would not see. God uses unlikely ways to spread the Word. I had met the Shah a few times, but I never had an opportunity to tell Him about Jesus. Since Amir was a close relative, I had high hopes that His Majesty and His family were members of God's army. Praise The Lord!

God continued His blessings on me: June 15, 1972, my beautiful daughter Joanna Dawn Walls was born. Valerie didn't bother to ask me about the fingers and toes. Jeff had doubts about the need for her in the beginning, but they formed a very deep love and relationship that would never fail. I then had the three most wonderful children in the world. I have prayed for them and their families every day since then because God has blessed me more than I deserve. He has brought me a long way since I first accepted His offer of forgiveness of my sins in 1958. I have failed Him numerous times, but He forgave me, and HE never failed me. I am assured that once saved, always saved, thus guaranteeing that I will soon be with Him in heaven. He still had work for me here on earth, no time for rest until He gives me perfect peace when He calls me home. Amen.

We invited Val's parents, Cliff & Erin Brady, to meet their new granddaughter, so they left Chris and Roger in Epping and flew to Tehran. We met them at the airport. They immediately started cuddling Jeff and Jo, then finally noticed that we were there too. Jeff was always on the move, so he was not in for too much cuddling. Once we arrived at our house and parked the car in the garage, they were amazed at our huge home. I realized that it was very large, but it then dawned that we could seat one hundred fifty people comfortably for dinner. (We had one hundred twenty-five or more for New Year's Eve dinner and celebrations with room to spare on December 31, 1972.) Cliff was very impressed with my new Dodge sedan and chauffeur. They spent thirty days spoiling the kids and seeing the sights, then they regretfully returned to England.

LOCKHEED EMPLOYMENT – Iran: 1967-1977

In 1973, Don B, Director Customer Service, called and asked if I would be able to meet him in Tripoli, Libya, and then to Kuwait. I was used to strange questions from people, so I said: "Sure," so I did a week later. Don was a good Christian and very likable; therefore, it was always a pleasure to work with him. Tripoli looked terrible compared to its condition when I was there on my last trip in 1967. Then everything was sparkling, and people had a spring in their walk. Now it was grimy, and people were more like zombies, with no hope. The hotels had lost their luster, very dismal since Colonel Gaddafi and a few young officers staged a coup and took control while King Idris and his family were out of the country in 1969. Gaddafi purchased a few C-130 aircraft and signed a contract with Lockheed Georgia for a ten-man support team. I recognized most of them. The resident representative Tom G was one of twenty men who had been hired upon graduating from high school for apprentice training. Tom G was the best of the lot. He was currently salary grade six and would start climbing. He had watched my career and knew that I had been in Libya a few times in the past, and wanted to know how much it had changed. The most accurate description was daylight to dark, what he expected me to say. All nine of his team looked like someone who had lost his best friend. Later, I quietly asked Tom and Don if they would mind going for a walk and give me a chance to try to raise the team morale. They deeply appreciated that. The team gathered around, and I listened to each tell me about his problems. Then I commiserated and assured them that the next assignment would be better, "just give your all to the job at hand to impress Tom and the customer with your performance and try to keep a smile on your face". "You have to adapt to the different country and its environmental differences but don't leave your Christian faith". "If this is not possible, talk with Tom and ask him to let you go home". "If you knuckle down and prove yourself, you might have a bright future with Lockheed. Go for it".

Jack B, who was the Lockheed rep for the Shah of Iran JetStar executive aircraft in Tehran, was to meet us in Kuwait, but Don had to cut his trip short. Our agent in Kuwait canceled his reservation at the Hilton Hotel, leaving the other two single rooms for Jack and me. Murphy's law stepped in: When we got to the check-in desk, I was told that our agent had canceled all reservations, and the hotel was fully booked. There were no vacancies in Kuwait. I read the riot act to our agent, then the desk clerk told me that the penthouse suite was available, and I said, "We will take it". The cost was six hundred US Dollars plus per night. I handed my American Express credit card to the clerk to pay for two nights. Baggage handlers led the way to the elevator, and it went directly to our suite, which was actually a house covering the entire top of the hotel. We had come up in a private elevator that is run by an operator. The suite had three large bedrooms, four bathrooms (two with hot tubs), two huge living areas, and unimaginable amenities. A place fit for a king or a redneck country boy from South Georgia. Jack kept looking at the living quarters and repeating that Lockheed is not going to like this. I told him not to sweat the small stuff; we had no choice; I paid the bill, and I am Lockheed in this area. Fifty years later, a South Georgia redneck would not be allowed to rent the suite.

LOCKHEED EMPLOYMENT – Iran: 1967-1977

Karl K, President of Lockheed Corporation, and his wife Lucy, made their first trip to see us. They came to our house for dinner, and he shared my love for Indian curry. He had his best curry that night. Joanna was just a baby, but Jeff was hyper-actively entertaining everyone. Karl was favorably impressed with my family and what I had accomplished. The Shah and generals had praised me, so Karl had big plans for me. He always insisted on having personal knowledge of managers and their families before promoting them to high management positions. I had given God thanks for all of His blessings and rightfully given Him the glory for what He had allowed me to do, but was about to be prideful. God was getting ready to remind me that only HE is worthy.

One of the men who worked for me had married a German Duchess who had a dachshund with a royal pedigree. The dog now had puppies, and they were going on vacation to USA and needed a trustworthy person to care for the animals. They knew that I wouldn't fall for that, so the so-called duchess offered Valerie the pick of the litter if she would care for the animals. The litter was as active as Jeffry, but were content in our smaller living room with the door closed. Karl and his wife were on a sofa in our extremely large living/dining area, and Val and I were facing them. Valerie never liked anyplace except dreary Pakistan with her friends dating back to India, so she was not as happy as I. We had tried to get into numerous activities to overcome this. I loved Iran and the citizens under the Shah's control, so this drove a bigger wedge between. Anyway, as I was swelling with pride, Jeff decided that his baby sister should join in; therefore, Val had to dash to prevent Jeff from dragging her out of the cot. Karl and his wife insisted on handing Jo back and forth, so they sat their drinks on the low table. Meantime, Jeff opened the door and released the six-pack of wild dogs that raced him back to include themselves in the fun and games. Our honored guests were trying to juggle Joanna and not step on puppies, while the mother dog sipped Karl's drink. Lucy passed Jo to Karl, then picked the dog up and was set to throw a touchdown, but the dog struck first by urinating down the front of Lucy's (had to be expensive) dress (Sounds impossible, but it is true). I knew that I would be fired or even worse, but what? The puppies and kids were secured, Val was desperately working to help sanitize Lucy's dress, and I was trying to be invisible, but Karl started laughing. He assured me that I would fit his plans because I had a great and fun-loving family. I thought that he had a weird sense of humor, but smiled. After the fiasco, we went to the dining table to partake of Indian curry that Valerie had cooked especially for them. They really enjoyed it and the hot condiments, thus assuring that I still had a job. Both of them liked our big house for entertainment and asked what we had planned for the year-end holidays. I told them that we expected one hundred twenty-five for New Year's Eve, which would include several Iranian officers and their wives, all of the Lockheed men and their wives in the Tehran area, Iran Air employees, several friends from India, Philippines, Australia, New Zealand, and locally. He thought that was a good plan and asked how we would acquire supplies. Val and I thought we would be able to find them locally, but he said someone in his office would buy the items and have them delivered.

Two weeks before New Year's Eve, three vice presidents had a need to visit us and decorate our home. They checked into

LOCKHEED EMPLOYMENT – Iran: 1967-1977

the Hilton and arrived in two taxi cabs. They unloaded six huge boxes and struggled to bring them in. I was kind enough to open the front door and watch them. They had decorations for the room and started hanging them without my assistance. These men had been pampered since birth and probably had never done a day of manual labor, but they had been especially motivated by someone. I knew the motivator. The boxes contained enough special plates, cups, napkins, etc., for two hundred people. They had noisemakers and everything needed for a bang-up celebration. There was a huge tough paper bag and roughly four hundred trinkets that were put inside the bag, which was attached by a thin rope to the ceiling. Just before midnight, each person would be issued a thin wooden stick, then I would give the bag a hard swing and jump back to avoid the sticks that were being swung. Once the bag was ruptured, four hundred trinkets would fly all over the area. Getting back to the job that three vice presidents were into: They finished unloading and decorating while Val and the cook prepared a delicious dinner. I told Hamas, my chauffeur, to take the empty boxes to his house (boxes were a blessing to the local population), then take his wife out for dinner and come back here. After dinner, we moved into our living area. I had two large tape recorders with surround sound speakers in the area. I had a wide range of good music for entertainment, but most people preferred to hear Val play the baby grand piano or her accordion and sing. Eventually, everyone started singing along and never wanted to quit. I enjoyed the music and good singing, but people like me should not spoil it. Our gift bearers shared my inability to sing but chimed in. The noise became unbearable to me while Val and her three male companions ruined my day. Val and I had known three years before we married that we were not compatible because I could not carry a note. I was good at math and physics while she excelled at music and the arts; never the two shall meet.

The following morning, I picked them up for a tour around Tehran and to military headquarters to meet the commander, General Khatami, who was also the Shah's brother-in-law, then to meet other officials. That night, we treated them for dinner at a swanky restaurant and took them to the hotel. They knew that their work trip to Iran had been well worthwhile. New Year's Eve arrived before we realized it! The four colonels and their wives were the first to arrive. The men had put Jeff in control for the night, and their wives were passing Jo around when the other guests started arriving thirty minutes later. I had a wet bar and had hired a bartender. My driver volunteered to help him. Val and the cook had purchased and cooked the food. We had hired two women to help with miscellaneous duties, and we also had seating for one hundred thirty people. I put a long play tape of Christmas music on, knowing that Lockheed reps would take it from there. We were ready for a good night with friends, and that's the way it went. This group was made up of every race, creed, and color, nine nationalities, nine religious beliefs, and an unknown variety of other beliefs. We greeted people as they arrived and told them to introduce themselves to others. No one sat down until dinner was announced. Everyone got involved with the cleanup, so it was only a few minutes before the tables and chairs were cleared, stacked, and out of the way. We dismissed the workers with double pay and all of the leftover food. I told

LOCKHEED EMPLOYMENT – Iran: 1967-1977

Hamas to take everyone home and come back three days later.

Trouble was waiting outside. While we were having fun, a snowstorm had dumped a foot of snow, and it was now sleeting. I could not see our walkway or the twenty steps down to the street level where my garage was located. I had a shed with snow shovels and bags of salt near the house. A few friends removed the snow and salted the area quickly. I knew Hamas and the workers would be okay once the garage door was open because the streets went rapidly downhill toward the city, meaning that it would be raining a couple of miles down toward Tehran. Since there were no handrails, I insisted on checking the steps first, but when my foot touched the top step, both feet jumped forward; my bottom didn't miss either of the about twenty steps on my rapid descent. I didn't want anyone to be hurt while trying to give aid to me, so I sprang up and shouted, "Be careful, the steps are slippery!" The only thing that was hurt was my pride. Jeff enjoyed my performance. One of the sing-along concerts was already underway, but the crowd was ready to use the sticks when I gave the paper bag a mighty swing at midnight. The bag burst, and the trinkets flew everywhere. Very quickly, all of the trinkets disappeared off the floor. Everyone then started hugging and shaking hands with their newfound friends. Tonight proved that all nations could get along if the ultra-rich and crooked politicians would get out of the way. No one was drunk and displayed brotherly love.

We made occasional vacation trips to Georgia, and I went there at least once a year for meetings, allowing more time with Ricky and my mother. Karl and Lucy returned in May

1974 with an organization chart for Lockheed Middle East Corporation. Norm Orwat, currently President of Lockheed Europe, was president; I was Vice President for all aircraft programs (more than thirteen hundred people would report to me); Sam S was Marketing Vice President; and someone from Lockheed Aircraft Services was Director of Administration. Norm was a retired USAF major general. He had been commander of SHAPE in Paris, France, for several years, with an outstanding reputation. We took over my current office building, and I would have the same office, secretary, driver, and everything else to please my friends in Iran. Norm Orwat will be here later this week to meet me and locate a home. Karl told me to consider what salary and benefits I wanted, then give the list to Norm. He will bring your list to my office in two weeks. "After you and I meet with the Shah after lunch, Lucy and I will have dinner with you and Valerie tonight" (He had called a few days before to ask that Val cook some more spicy curry). "We will spend the night at the hotel, then fly back to Burbank so I can assure that your requests will be fulfilled". I didn't doubt that everything would go as he said. I knew that I had been blessed beyond my wildest dreams and should have bowed and thanked him for the generosity. Instead, I said, "Thank you for your trust and generosity, BUT I have been overseas for fifteen years, and would like to go back to work in Georgia on Davy Crockett's staff". I never wanted to have a chill like I instantly felt. Karl said, "Are you telling me that you and Dave prefer to be fired instead of you accepting a job that others would die for?" I swiftly tried to convince him that I meant to thank him for his blessings. He already knew

LOCKHEED EMPLOYMENT – Iran: 1967-1977

that he had trouble understanding South Georgia Rednecks. That gave me a warm feeling!

The Shah thanked Karl and said that he wants to buy ten C-5 Galaxy aircraft. He knew it would be expensive to start up production, so he was willing to pay two billion dollars to cover the startup. Several other countries wanted the Galaxy, so Karl assured him that I would have the contract within a week. The lawyer-driven contracts people never operate that rapidly unless Karl speaks. They started a 24/7 work week that afternoon, and it was in my hands a few hours under the deadline. Norm arrived, and we clicked immediately. He had married a very beautiful French woman of nobility, although the French had disbanded the nobles. Val and I became their closest friends. He didn't want to move from Europe to the Middle East and had voiced his desires to Karl as I had, and Karl gave him the same offer that I received. All four of us thought this was much funnier than it really was, but knew we were in the same boat.

Upon receipt of the C-5 contract, I went directly to the Ministry of War. As always, I had to pretend to enjoy a cup of hot tea while the vice minister ignored the contract. When I had forced down the tea, he told me that something had gone wrong, and His Majesty ordered him to go to the Pentagon and correct it. I felt deadly "OH NO" chills! He said, "Don't worry, come back the day after tomorrow, and I'll sign it". I said, "Thank you, Sir". It was definitely the time to worry. I thanked the Lord that I hadn't had a heart attack or worse after the situations that I had been through in my life. Of course, not many people have to be forced to be vice president of a large corporation before his forty-first

120

birthday. Guess I have to suffer through it. I was in my office on the phone with Dave Crockett soon after the meeting. He agreed to call the DC office. Karl was away: Don't know where... Two days later, the minister informed me that Lockheed had not asked for permission to use the C-5 tooling, and the Pentagon was angry with Lockheed. The tooling was now being destroyed. (That was a super stupid decision by some super stupid general.) The USAF and our allies needed the C-5. Lockheed and I had lost face with the Shah and would never get another contract for anything.

The British Ambassador invited Val and me to the New Year's Eve celebrations at the embassy, so I had to purchase a tuxedo or have one tailor-made. I had one tailored for the same thing in Pakistan, but only God knows what happened to it. The ambassador and his entourage greeted us and chatted for a while, then he said, "Bill, I can't place your accent, are you Australian or Canadian?" That gave Valerie her first healthy laugh in ages. She jumped in and answered the question much clearer than I wanted. "No, sir" would be perfect, but that was not in her reply. She had to explain that my speech problem derived from my childhood in South Georgia. The ambassador said, "I see". Interpreted, this meant that he had no idea about what that meant other than that I was a yankee. The British are not well educated: they don't know the difference between Yankee and Rebel. At midnight, the Royal Scottish Guard wearing miniskirts and long hose terrorized me with their bagpipes as they piped in their favorite dinner, Haggis, which is the Gaelic word for sheep's pluck, which means heart, lungs, and liver; YUCKY! I slid my helping to Val and tried to get a stiff upper lip and keep my nose in the air. These people should try a plate of

LOCKHEED EMPLOYMENT – Iran: 1967-1977

my mother's southern cooking. I pitied people who had to eat swine slop.

One day in 1975, Dave Crockett called and said, "I have bad news (I already had bad news, but he really had bad news for me). The US Congress is sending a summons to you to answer charges of aiding and abetting bribery of foreign government officials. You are not allowed any legal defense or advice; you are guilty until you prove innocence and must answer every question, no 5th Amendment rights. (Violation of my constitutional rights; only Congress is allowed to get away with this.) The manager of government sales and manager of commercial sales will appear before Congress, and you will be tried by four Congress-appointed lawyers in Paris, France. (This probably was not the right time to remind Dave that I don't like France.) I will receive the summons by special delivery and sign for it, then I must appear on time or go to jail. Sorry, Bill. Have a good day". The only problems I had with this was that I had to make an unnecessary trip to France and debate against ambulance chasers. Being a born-again Christian, I knew that God's will would be done. God was with me, so no one could prevail against His Will.

I signed to accept the summons, discovering that I would have to face the mod squad eight hours on Monday and again on Tuesday, starting two weeks from that day. I called my travel agent and made reservations for first-class flights to Paris, then to London and back to Tehran, and for a suite in the Paris Hilton Hotel for three nights. The Farnborough Air Show was being held while I was being hung, so Dave had made a reservation for me at the prestigious Inn on the Park

Hotel in London. He and the president of Lockheed Georgia and several other officials would be at the air show and had a strong interest in the outcome of my trial. I didn't need the suite in Paris for Tuesday night but thought I would take the time to relax and make rational plans for the future based on God's will. I had previously stayed at the Paris Hilton, which was very close to the Eiffel Tower. A small group of Lockheed Europe had a suite of offices three blocks from the Tower. It was set up to support officials from all Lockheed offices on business in France. I had used the conference room and secretary twice before. I had always walked to and from the office. My case was going to be tried in a large conference room across the street from the Lockheed office.

I arrived five minutes early but waited before opening the door. All four of the accusers came toward me with smiles. The leader had his hand stretched out and said, "Mr. Walls?" I ignored his outstretched hand and replied, "Who were you expecting, Smokey Bear?" They insisted that we had to keep a friendly atmosphere and work together. Working together would not fit my plans, so I suggested that we get the show on the road. They turned the cameras and sound on and focused floodlights on my eyes, but I had dark sunglasses with reflective lenses that offset that. That displeased them, according to my plans. I couldn't read anything; neither could they tell when I was asleep. They also were upset when I kept yawning and occasionally let my head fall over. I seldom did that because I did not want to be charged with the contempt I had. They had several leather file cases with every message I had sent, many were coded, but they had our code book and flashed some documents with decoded words to intimidate me. I was pleased to inform them that

LOCKHEED EMPLOYMENT – Iran: 1967-1977

they had been coded to slow down people who had no need to know what was being said. They knew more about my life than I did, so they had to refresh my memory. My memory was not so good now that I was forty. Before lunch, they were upset that it was necessary to remind me that they had messages that I couldn't seem to remember and had no recollection of some things that I had been involved in. They had data that must have come from... CIA? Surely Not! They had to ask why I went through two years of law school and changed to physics. They knew it was a mistake to pose that question when I replied that I found that I was not a good liar. No one understands my sense of humor. I had offended them without breaking a law.

I insisted on presenting my case when the afternoon session began; they might never regroup, so I was allowed to take the floor. I carefully explained in a way that even lawyers could understand. Some countries such as Saudi Arabia insist that any company willing or wanting to do business must have an agent to represent them. There is a language barrier, so the agent must translate and explain the lawyer language to their satisfaction. The country will only allow certified agents, and there is only one agent in Saudi Arabia. The agent's fee is ten percent of the contract price. The seller is authorized to add ten percent to the contract price and then pay the agent after the seller receives full payment. The company and shareholders are happy, the agent is happy, and the country is pleased that they didn't have to pay an agent for a year for working two months. We never wanted an agent, and most countries don't tolerate it. Furthermore, I knew of the sales but was never involved with any procedures. My job was to teach people how to maintain the aircraft after delivery. When an employer hires a man to work, the worker is not obligated to tell his employer how he spent the money. No law has been broken, shareholders lost no money. Crooked politicians take bribes and sell classified documents and prosecute innocent people for the crimes they committed. (This would be verified when Donald Trump was prosecuted to distract attention away from "Someone" who sold classified documents to China.) I was found not guilty. I walked to my hotel and canceled the room for the next night, then changed my flight to London accordingly. I checked into the Inn on the Park hotel at the same time Lockheed executives were returning from the air show. Davy Crockett and Bob O, President of Lockheed Georgia, guided me to a quiet conference room where I related the details and verdict of my "interview". They were elated. I went with them to the Farnborough Air Show the next day and dined with them that night.

The fun and festivities were over, and I took the Iran Air direct flight to Tehran the following morning. Norm and I worked in our new jobs a few more days, then discovered that Karl K had taken early retirement. It seemed strange that he had not notified us and had not returned my calls. During my investigation, I did learn that the two sales managers had been terminated. They had done nothing wrong, but no one knew anything. Finally, we got in touch with the new president and talked with him on a conference call. He thought Karl would enjoy retirement and told us to keep up the good work. This was getting creepy. We still did not want our jobs, so we prepared a letter requesting that Lockheed Middle East Corporation be dissolved. The president approved it. Norm had enough and retired. I took an

LOCKHEED EMPLOYMENT – Iran: 1967-1977

enormous pay cut and realized that my career was dead. When a person resigns from a position like that, he will never be considered again. I kept my office, secretary, car, and driver and went back to work as program manager.

The Boeing Program manager called and asked me to congratulate him; the Shah had signed a contract with Boeing to convert ten 747 aircraft to cargo aircraft so he does not need C-5. I told him that the 747 cannot be used without special loading and unloading, and only a C-5 can carry that equipment. "Is Boeing going to provide ten C-5s?" I laughed and hung up. They did deliver ten 747 cargo aircraft to Iran, and C-5s delivered the loading equipment. Someone failed to do his homework. I never heard from Boeing or the Shah again. I continued my duties and entertainment; also going on business trips to the home office and vacations to the US in order to keep my children in touch and also to see my aging mother, but felt terrible about our inability to restart the C-5 program.

In January 1977, peanut farmer Jimmy Carter walked into the White House with weird plans. He replaced USA manufactured cars used by government agencies with worthless Russian Yugos; cut military spending and everything to destroy our economy. Hyperinflation began, service stations ran out of fuel, aircraft could not fly due to lack of money for fuel and spare parts; ammunition was not available, etc., so we could not fight a war. Ted Turner was a billionaire who made a fortune on advertisements and investments. His headquarters were in Atlanta. Jimmy Carter had a peanut farm in South Georgia and bragged about teaching Sunday school. It was a strange relationship, but

Ted put him in the White House. We saw them and their families together at Atlanta Braves baseball games. Ted owned the Braves and either the Falcons Football Team or the Hawks Basketball Team. He owned CNN, Turner Broadcasting, and a few more TV and Radio Stations. He was President Carter's puppet master, or so it seemed to me.

Our fabulous president apparently noticed that some of our best allies prospered by keeping the radicals under control, so he felt it was his duty to remove the leaders and let the radical American and Israeli-hating Muslims get back in control. He was busy polishing his halo and destroying the USA, so he sent a four-star general (I will not release his name) and a large entourage to Iran, and he told the Shah that he must give the radicals freedom to assemble and demonstrate. The CIA had put the Shah's father in power after World War 2 to keep stability in the area. The radical Ayatollahs had ruled Persia for hundreds of years. Shah Pahlavi had received the throne when his father died. He refused to be crowned before he used the enormous resources to build schools, hospitals, housing, and other necessities for the citizens. He banned the veil for women and gave them equal rights with men. Everyone got free education, and the country had come out of the dark ages. The Shah was of the Sunni sect of Islam, only ten percent of the Iran population. Ayatollah Khomeini was supreme leader of the radical Shias, which were eighty-eight percent of the population. Khomeini and his tribe believed the women should wear the Burqa and be treated like cattle. When the Shah educated girls and freed them from bondage, Khomeini and his henchmen rebelled and attempted to overthrow the Shah. The Ayatollah was exiled to France, and the Shias and

LOCKHEED EMPLOYMENT – Iran: 1967-1977

Sunnis lived together in harmony. Iran imported fresh fruit and vegetables from Israel and supplied Israel with oil even during the Six-Day War when I was in Libya and the Yom Kippur War when I was in Iran. Israeli officials confirmed the facts when I visited Tel Aviv on several occasions. Iran bought all of their arms, aircraft, training, and supplies from the USA and paid cash. Iran had about one hundred billion dollars in US banks to cover future purchases. Some is still in the banks, but in 2023 and 24, President Biden released several billion to the ayatollahs so they could develop nuclear bombs and finance Hamas and other terrorist radicals' attacks on Israel. The Shah was the strongest and best ally of all times for the USA and Israel. The Democrat candidates for president and vice president in 2024 and a large number of their supporters are demonstrating and shouting, "Death to America and Death to Israel". This is in perfect sync with the current ayatollah.

Remaining faithful to the US, Shah Pahlavi concurred with Radical Carter's wishes. Chaos erupted; rioters started killing indiscriminately, and they attacked military headquarters. The Shah had ordered the police and military to stand down. The current military commander opened the gates, and the rioters hung the commander, then opened the armory and took all guns and ammunition out to create further havoc. My employees and I watched this play out on television. The Shah announced that he would go into exile in France the next day. Davy Crockett called and told me to take my family anywhere in Europe that I chose to keep them safe and then return to Iran. General Amir F moved his family to England, and I moved my family to Cambridge, England, where Sir Arthur Marshall was happy to give me a large office next door to his. We found a new large Georgian house for rent in Cambridge. As soon as the Shah left for exile in Paris, Ayatollah Khomeini left Paris and flew to Iran; things quieted down for a few days. Amir went back to Iran, but I stayed in England for several weeks to settle my family in. I bought two new cars from one of Sir Arthur's forty-three auto sales and service agencies and traveled to several countries to represent Dave C.

Chapter 9
Operating out of England - 1977-1981

As Iranian Air Force General Amir F had planned, he came back to England and moved his family to Paris, but came to my office first to tell me what had happened. Khomeini had lured officials who had close ties to the Shah back to Iran to work with his regime for reconstruction. Amir was given the job as Director of Iran Airlines, and others were given similar positions, but some stayed in France where they were working to overthrow Khomeini. After everything appeared that Khomeini was serious, he collected their passports in order to issue new ones with the new title "Islamic Republic of Iran" on them. No one wanted the new title but had to surrender the passports. A few days later, Amir called his office to ask why his driver had not been there to pick him up, and the male receptionist told him that his car was on the way and wanted to confirm that he was at home. He said that he was, then picked up a backpack and ran out the back door and across the street to his sister's house. His sister and her husband were with the Shah in Paris. He peeked out the window and watched a truckload of soldiers destroy his home with machine guns. The gunmen knew that no one could survive that barrage, and neighbors had gathered to observe the strange happenings, so they sped away. One of the neighbors let Amir hide in the back seat of his SUV while he drove up a small road into the Alborz Mountain range. Then he got out and hiked across the mountain and through an unmanned area of the border with Turkey. Amir then gave an official a big handful of large denominations of US Dollars to get him onto a direct flight to London. He received amnesty for thirty days in England, then would be required to leave the United Kingdom.

Ayatollah Khomeini had given orders to assassinate everyone affiliated with the Shah, so I tried to get Amir to seek asylum in Marietta, Georgia, where numerous of our friends had fled to. I could help him and his family there, but he was determined to work with the Shah and their contacts in France. He pleaded for me to join them, but I had no desire to return to Paris. I flew to Tehran the next day and checked into the new Intercontinental Hotel. All of the Lockheed Georgia personnel in Tehran met me in my office. John W was my trusted friend and the man in charge when I was away. I told everyone that decisions had been made to charter two aircraft to move them to Atlanta. They and their family members were allowed two suitcases each, nothing else, and must be at the airport three days from then. John was a retired USAF Chief Master Sergeant and felt that things would settle down, but the other people started dancing and making merry. All of the twenty Lockheed employees in Shiraz were ready to go. My treasurer and bookkeeper wrote nice termination checks to my secretary and driver. I locked the building and handed the keys to John. My secretary and I wished each other a fond farewell; all of the reps left in their cars to help their wives pack, and my driver and I stopped at the bazaar to purchase twenty pounds of pistachio nuts. Iran grows the best in the world. I treated Les Jayasinghe's family and our mutual friends to dinner. They were still working for Iran Airlines. They told me General Amir F had taken over as director of the airline, but had suddenly disappeared. I

Operating out of England – 1977-1981

suggested that he might have taken a vacation, but they didn't buy that. Everyone wanted to know about Valerie, Jeff, and Jo; what we are doing. We knew that we would never be in touch again, so it was a sad farewell when we parted. I heard gunshots and explosions at a distance throughout the next eighteen hours as Khomeini's enemies were dying. Twelve of my friends and the Shah's supporters lived near Atlanta, but many others made the mistake of staying in Iran or of being lured back. A very large number were also dying because of their faith in Jesus Christ. Others would never denounce Christ, so they would be killed without mercy. This would continue well after the Shah's supporters were exterminated because radical Islam hates Christians and Jews. Some that I had witnessed to were being slaughtered. Gunfire and explosions were now up close and all across the country until my team flew out to Atlanta, and I boarded my flight to London. I never saw any of my Christian friends or military friends again. The Shah and Amir and others with them in France must have died there. The Shah's son was on the news, Fox News (?) in 2024. He was about twelve the last time I saw him in Tehran. He has lived through the slaughter, so I believe he and I might be the only two left who know all of the facts. In 2024, I will be approaching my ninety-second birthday; otherwise, I would force myself to fly to France and work with him.

Back to the present, I made a ten-week trip to Africa to greet leaders in Morocco, Niger, Nigeria, Cameroon, Ivory Coast, Zaire, and South Africa. I also went to Turkey, Lebanon, Kuwait, India, and Israel in the Middle East. I made two trips to Denmark, Norway, Sweden, Holland, Germany, Luxembourg, Monaco, Italy, Austria, Spain, France, and

Belgium in Europe. In my spare time, I made trips to the RAF C-130 Base, to Logistics Command Headquarters, and the Ministry of Defense in England.

Actually, I made four trips to Turkey over a period of about fourteen years. The first time was when I was leaving Libya on a US Air Force C-130H and heading for Spain. The flight crew said that I should become acquainted with Turkey, so we landed at the US Air Base at Incirlik, Turkey, and spent two days helping me to further my education. I probably learned a lot, but only remember the impossible Limbo Dance at the nightclub. A tall man (had to be reptilian) came onto the stage while the Limbo music and bright lights highlighted the area. A man and woman set the bar at fifteen inches and placed a lit candle under it. The weird man leaned backwards and actually walked back under the bar and kept going like a cobra until his entire body had cleared the flame. To clarify: his head turned ninety degrees to the right, causing his right ear to pass over the flame while his left ear cleared the bottom of the bar. His feet were under his hips as he continued the journey. His upper body slowly rose, and his knees were at the same elevation as his hips when he slow-walked until his entire body cleared and he was standing upright. Impossible, you say, and I totally agree, but a four-man C-130 flight crew knew that it was true.

The next two trips to Turkey were during the times that I lived in Cambridge, England. I would fly into Ankara, and a Lt. General from Turkish Air Force Headquarters (it would not be prudent if I mentioned that he was the air force commander) took me in his chauffeur-driven limo to Kayseri in a remote area in the interior. The chauffeur was also a

Operating out of England – 1977-1981

heavily armed bodyguard. The general's friend was the commander of Logistics and also a Lt. General who was responsible for buying and selling in Turkey. We always had dinner at his home. There was no hanky-panky involved, but simply what Lockheed could do to support their C-130 aircraft as Turkey fought along with the USA in skirmishes with radical Islamic countries, which was somewhat like Iran had done pre-Jimmy Carter. This made us personal blood brothers. Kayseri was a small village with one tiny wannabe hotel. There is no way in English or Arabic to describe the hotel or food, but I was happy to spend a night conferring with Allies like these two generals. God had blessed me with a perfect body that would allow me to thrive in conditions that would be fatal for most Americans. The air force commander always took a meandering trip to and from Kayseri to show me all of the early Christian sights that few tourists have even heard about, although some go to a few areas that Turkish guides lead. My personal guide knew everything and was well versed. There are two underground cities. The smaller one was permanently closed due to cave-ins, and the other one was dug by hand on top of a small mountain by Christians. The Christians would be able to see Arabic armies approaching, thus allowing them to go into the huge six-story "city" with all of their animals and possessions. They removed all evidence that could reveal that people had been there, and after the last person walked in a crouched position through the small opening, he would pull a lever that allowed a very large rock to roll about three feet downhill and seal the entrance. They had spring-fed pools of pure water for the humans and animals. Cooking smoke was channeled through natural openings and disappeared without sight or scent. There was no food or water, so the Arabs did not linger. The city had a spiral staircase down six flights. Everyone, including I, had to be in good physical condition to walk down and back up. The site was closed for the winter, and no one was allowed near except a general like my new friend. He ordered the caretakers to open and give me a fully guided tour, then they were overjoyed to please him. The general would not allow me to give a "tip" but he handed all of the workers a generous bonus. We also checked out the Christian Churches and homes in mountains, which were caves. I was given a guided tour through most of Turkey, even to the largest mosque that was located in Istanbul. Istanbul is in Europe, whereas the rest of Turkey is in Asia.

The fourth and final visit was after I retired from Lockheed and worked as an International Aircraft marketing consultant. The Air Force commander refused to get involved since I was then there to sell parts. They still welcomed me in Kayseri, though. I had to ride from Ankara in a bus, but still had dinner at the home of the Logistics Commander. He took all the C-130 parts business away from Y and bought it from me at X. In turn, I was asked to sell the Turkish Air Force fleet of C-47 aircraft. They knew, as I did, that there was no market for the old C-47 aircraft. When I went through the Los Angeles airport on the way home from my round-the-world trip, Red Flags came up when I handed my passport to the immigration officer. He demanded to know why I continued making trips to Turkey. "Do you know anyone or do business there?" I had two answers: "Yes, and it's none of your business!" He summoned me to an office to answer to a man who was a CIA Agent without a

Operating out of England – 1977-1981

doubt. I gave him the same answer and hurt his feelings. He threatened me, and I took my cell phone out and offered to call a couple of congressmen on the oversight committee because I had not broken any laws and was simply being harassed. He glared at me and waved me out. I grinned and slowly strolled out. (Don't try this now.)

During my time at Marshall Aerospace, I had lunch in the executive dining room with Sir Arthur Marshall and his son Sir Michael Marshall; Peter Hederwick, Managing Director of Marshall Aerospace, and all of Sir Arthur's staff. Sir Arthur had inherited a small auto garage in Cambridge and used hard work and integrity to amass a fortune. He now owned forty-three auto sales and service agencies and several distributorships; He also owned the Cambridge Airport and flying club. Marshall Aerospace (Lockheed C-130 & L-100 Aircraft and Cessna Citation Aircraft overhaul facilities) were at the airport; He also owned a large farm with a small mansion* on it. *(Very large old house in good condition.); He owned a Cessna Citation executive jet, and he was the senior pilot; He had a large Rolls Royce and chauffeur, and a large Cadillac Sedan. Sir Arthur was a workaholic with great charisma, one of the richest men and without doubt the most powerful person in Great Britain. All of the nobility sought his advice.

One day, I came out of my office the moment he and Prime Minister Margaret Thatcher stepped out of his doorway. The prime minister looked for UFOs while Sir Arthur and I had a short greeting. The same thing occurred a few months later when he and Prince Charles, now King Charles, bumped into me. Too bad Sir Arthur didn't tell him to clean up his act and quit cheating on Princess Diana by shacking up with a married woman. No one has ever accused British Nobles of having morals or integrity. Alley cats are fun seekers, no pun intended! Maybe a wee bit. Sir Arthur and Lady Marshall invited Valerie and me for dinner, and we were favorably impressed with their beautiful home and the two of them. They were married at a young age and were dedicated to one another all of their lives. They were not pretentious and did not try to impress anyone, but were billionaires and seemed like a South Georgia farm couple. Sir Arthur and I had a close relationship until the last time I saw him in the 1990s. No one knew of anyone who had been invited to their home before this or afterwards. I had to wonder why they invited a redneck like me. We tried to reciprocate, but they never attended dinner functions. Sir Michael Marshall and Peter Hedderwick and their wives never declined, though, and we were invited to their homes also.

During 1979, I made two trips to all of the European countries and to Morocco in North Africa, and one swing around the Middle East. Lockheed officials and peons now knew from my reports about Sir Arthur, and several sought a need to see me. I ignored most of them, but welcomed a few who had a reason. The president of Lockheed Georgia and two vice presidents brought their wives to Cambridge. All of us ate lunch with Sir Arthur and his staff in the executive dining room, after which Sir Arthur gave a guided tour of the facilities. Val and I spent the next two days showing them around London. All of this was so productive that I was given a commendation. That made my day! With that and two dollars, I could buy a lousy cup of English tea, while being snubbed by the waitress. We took a vacation to

Operating out of England – 1977-1981

see Ricky and my mother but had no reason to drop into my home office. I bought my mother a round-trip ticket to London, and she began the trip of her life. She had lived in Alabama, Georgia, and Florida all of her life and had never flown. She had a window seat and was overjoyed. When we took a train through London and up to Cambridge, she soaked everything in. I asked what she thought of the flight, and she really enjoyed it but got cold because the man in front of her kept his window down. I tried to explain that the windows would not go down, but had to concede that she was right when she carefully told me that I didn't know what I was saying. We spent four weeks showing her Buckingham Palace and Changing of the Guard; Houses of Parliament; Big Ben; the Crown Jewels; Thames River, and much more in London. We used taxi cabs, double-deck buses, underground railway, and trains to give her a feel for the things that she saw. We drove through villages, towns, and back roads of England, Wales, and Scotland. We took photos of her at each event, then bought a beautiful white leather scrapbook. Valerie spent countless hours posting the pictures and writing the details under each one. My brother Dewitt and his wife Pauline met her at the airport in Atlanta and took her home. She showed the scrapbook to them and couldn't stop talking about her trip, so Dewitt and Pauline called and said that they would like to go to the same places. They flew over, and we took them on the same tours. As soon as they returned home, our sister Mildred wanted equal treatment.

Getting back to Jeff and Jo; shortly after our arrival in England, they were enrolled in St. John's College School. The schools are set up totally different from the ones in the USA (quaint and weird), so I will just use grades. Jeff was in the fourth grade, and Jo entered first grade. St. Johns was a private school. Jo's school building was a block away from Jeff's school. When I was not traveling internationally, I would drop them off in the morning on the way to my office and pick them up on the way home. When I traveled, Valerie handled the shuttle business.

When I traveled to corporate headquarters in California, I asked Lockheed Georgia to look at the possibility of setting up a center for aircraft overhaul and for components in Indonesia. Karl K had retired, but they recalled the job I had done for aircraft overhaul in Iran. They wanted me to take a sales manager and finance manager from Lockheed Georgia with me to Jakarta. Just what I needed: a salesman and a bean counter. I knew who would do the entire job, but said, "Okay, I'll get a round-trip ticket and meet them in Jakarta". But, I was asked to go to Georgia for a briefing, lead the two to Jakarta, make all assessments, and come back to Georgia for debriefing. This really made sense; I would have a seventeen-hour time change to Indonesia and a seventeen-hour time change back to England. Who would do the briefing and debriefing? Me, of course. Someone in his rocking chair would snooze; therefore, I would have to put it in writing. Only God knows why I am tolerating this! Away I went.

The finance manager was from South Georgia and a good old boy like me, and this would be his first trip overseas. The sales manager had replaced my good friend who had been fired by Congress because of a false claim of bribery. The Director of Product Support and Logistics would receive my briefing and receive my new written report, then send it

Operating out of England – 1977-1981

under his heading to the president of the corporation and president of Lockheed Georgia. That should give him all kinds of rewards if they liked it, but politics. The blame would be given to me if they didn't like it. We stopped in Tokyo on the way over and in Hong Kong on the way back. Everyone loved a couple of days in Hong Kong for shopping. Lockheed officials stayed in the super luxury Peninsula Hotel. A chauffeur-driven Rolls Royce picks you up at the airport and takes you to the colonial-style hotel where you are greeted by a British gentleman wearing a large top hat and a stiff upper lip. There are no charges for the services, but the driver, greeter, baggage handlers, and service personnel at that hotel expected a very large tip in US green dollar bills. Our currency was better than gold in those days. But we are currently departing Tokyo and on the way to Jakarta. I am more engrossed in thinking about Bali and Nina than my workdays in Indonesia. I knew that Nina would not welcome me again, and I certainly did not want to endanger her and her mother by driving out to their location. It was not the time to think about the past. Lockheed personnel did not live and work there any longer. Indonesia wanted to buy new C-130s to replace their aging fleet of C-130s, but the State Department and Congress blocked the sale because the country required an agent. Indonesia had no choice other than the worthless French Transall two-engine cargo aircraft. France had built it to compete with the C-130, but it would not fill their needs, so the French Air Force bought C-130s. Indonesia paid double the price for something that did not fill their requirements. The French unloaded their cargo aircraft and had enough money to buy C-130s and pay bribes in addition to legal agent fees. That was absolutely okay with our double-standard government. Some of our officials openly receive "donations" from our enemies because a few receive huge bribes under the table. (I'll wash your hands if you'll wash mine. Quid Pro Quo.) Great for some politicians but destroys hard-working honest tax-paying citizens.

Dictator General Sukarno had been overthrown by country lover Suharto. The country was beautiful and thriving. Everyone had incomes, homes, food, and transportation. Streets, water, sewage, and electricity were in perfect condition and operation. There were no beggars or prostitutes on the streets. Bigger and better hotels, homes, apartments, condos, and service stations were in abundance. Absolutely amazing. We checked into the new luxury Hilton Hotel. We had my favorite dinner in Indonesia; Nasi Goreng (precooked basmati rice which is mixed with meat and vegetables and then fried). I drool when I think of it because it would be a good substitute for Indian chicken vindaloo curry even though it isn't spicy. The buffet breakfast at the Hilton had American-style food but also included Nasi Goreng with lightly fried eggs on top. Fabulous, but my cohorts were like most American travelers; they had to have American hillbilly food. Rednecks like I love anything except the innards of animals (bah humbug).

A Russian bus took us to the old C-130, Old Russian, new worthless French Transall aircraft air base where the only people in sight were a large number of Russians with their hireling Cubans, unworthy Frenchmen, and a smattering of Indonesians. Our ignorant government believed that wounds would be healed if Lockheed would spend several million

Operating out of England – 1977-1981

dollars to set up overhaul facilities and train Frenchmen, Russians, and Cubans to operate everything. Duh. Sounds good to a lot of weird people, but I am always ready to offend them. I could have filed the report with a short verbal sentence, but decided to make it in a way that even politicians might understand. I took several pictures in and around the area that should be enough for now. I did not say hello or goodbye to the very interested onlookers. I told the Indonesian officer that came with us that things were looking good, which made him happy, and he could file a good report to officials. They probably would send me to Bali for another two-week vacation, but I had to prepare a good report. My co-travelers kept wondering how we were doing with the report but understood that I was thinking. We spent a week there as I showed them around Jakarta and dined at excellent restaurants where they had their favorite food and I had mine. We stopped in Hong Kong and finally returned to Marietta. I handed my handwritten report to the director of Product Support and Logistics and told him that it would be good if he would add to it and have his secretary type it before we made a formal report to the president. He agreed, and I departed to pick up Ricky and go see my mother/his grandmother on our farm. We had a merry time, but I had to leave.

The director allowed me to pass out copies of "our" report to the president, vice president for finance, manager of finance, director of marketing, and sales manager. I then made a verbal presentation including the photos that I had taken and explained that it would cost more than five million dollars to renovate the hangar and shops and buy test equipment. An additional cost would be incurred to train personnel. The hostile relationship would prohibit most countries from sending aircraft and components for overhaul, and finally, Russia and France would take over. I felt that it would be a loser, and everyone heartily agreed. When I arrived in London, my body clock was somewhere around Hawaii. My time with Ricky and my mother was a blessing, but it was also great to be back with Jeff and Jo.

In November of 1979, Ayatollah Khomeini knew that the wimp in the White House was afraid to intervene, so his radicals climbed over the walls of the U.S. Embassy in Tehran and held the Americans hostage for 444 days. The ambassador and a few others had already evacuated, but the Charge d'Affairs and about forty-five staff were separated into separate rooms. Each one was bound and blindfolded, and two guards were in each room with explosives and were heavily armed, so rescue was impossible. Ronald Regan was campaigning for President in 1980, so Carter had to perform a miracle and rescue the hostages or be defeated by Regan. That would cause the deaths of hostages and rescuers, but Carter and his favorite general did not bother to confer with people who had been in the embassy, so they sent four special C-130 aircraft and about the same number of Apache helicopters to land in the Iranian desert in the middle of the night. The plan was to load the helicopters with troops and have them slide down ropes into the embassy yard and surprise the guards. A first-grade student would nix that. Landing in the dark with one aircraft is tricky, but this was chaotic. A couple of aircraft and helicopters were destroyed, and an unknown number of people were killed or wounded. The survivors picked up the dead and wounded and escaped. The embassy hostages were held until Regan took office, but

Operating out of England – 1977-1981

they were released the moment Ronald Regan was sworn in. The first week of January 1981, after destroying Carter in the election, we went from the worst president to one of the best ever.

Russia had planned to conquer all of Africa and the Middle East to obtain diamond sources, oil, and minerals, and was struggling to accomplish anything until Carter handed the region to the KGB. At the time Carter handed Iran to Russia, he did the same to South Africa, Rhodesia, Zaire, Angola, and many others. Much worse than a major war. I continued traveling to Europe and Asia and to Morocco in Africa until 1981. I had visited the Moroccan Air Force each year since 1977, so I was acquainted with people at headquarters and the C-130 air base. The best acquaintances were the minister of defense and the military commander. Both of them had been captains in the air force and were C-130 pilots before the minister of defense and the military commander tried to overthrow the king. The two captains led a counter coup d'etat and either killed or arrested the attackers. All of the plotters were executed by a firing squad, and my two friends were given the jobs of minister and commander. I had met them in the Azores while working for Air Rescue and Recovery. They were flying a C-130 on the way from the USA to Morocco and had to land at Lajes AB because of a radio problem. I was on site and corrected their problem; therefore, they became my friends, and all doors were open to me. Simply because all of us loved the C-130 aircraft. Unbelievable but true.

In 1981, Bob O, President of Lockheed Martin, and I decided that I should move back to Georgia in order to let Jeff and Jo secure their citizenship. It was necessary since they were born outside the USA and Valerie was born in India. I could have waited a few more years, but a few people were still concerned about what was still happening to everyone who had been associated with the Shah. I did not believe that there was any problem since I was simply a foreigner who had been there and certainly was not a decision maker. I didn't object to being back near Ricky, and Jeff and Jo would also be there. Sir Arthur Marshall gave me a large farewell party in his executive dining room and gave me three cherished gifts: a solid silver Armada dish, a Claret jug, and a painting. The painting was of a Royal Air Force C-130 just after takeoff with me sitting on top with a "How to fix an aircraft" book spread in front of me. Sir Arthur was standing on the ground of his airport waving bye-bye. The gifts wouldn't be worth much on the market, but were their weight in gold because Sir Arthur had never given those to anyone else!

Chapter 10
Lockheed Employment - 1981-1990

President Bob O asked me to set up and operate a program, to write a letter to each owner/operator of the C-130/L-100 Hercules aircraft, soliciting his comments regarding satisfactions or complaints. Even though I would lose a lot of money on fringe benefits and prestige, it would be worth it all by being back in the USA with my family in OUR home. Ricky had married, and I had the pleasure of flying back home to attend his wedding to Julie Rhadans. I could not have chosen anyone better; she was not only beautiful but was from a God-loving family. This was a perfect marriage. Ricky had attended Emory University and received a Bachelor's Degree in chemistry for pre-medical and had gone another year for additional credits. He and Julie were at the University of Georgia where he would soon have a PhD, and Julie would earn a Bachelor's Degree in Math. Although I would not have full time with them, I would still be able to see them occasionally.

I took a long vacation to find a home and furnish it. I bought a full-size Chevrolet Impala Sedan for myself. Val was not interested in a vehicle, but finally agreed to drive one if I could get something small. I refused to purchase a foreign-made vehicle, but discovered that Chevrolet built a medium-size station wagon that she reluctantly accepted. Our transportation problem was solved; now we were looking for a new brick house in a nice neighborhood, which was difficult. When I went to work at Lockheed in June 1955, there were about two hundred fifty thousand people in metro Atlanta, and now the number was more than four million and rapidly growing. We tried two different real estate agents, and neither was very helpful. The houses were in terrible locations, and the neighborhoods were deplorable, so we started cruising around on our own and were about to despair until I turned into a street that continued a short distance and turned left for a short distance and came to a dead end. People were on the sidewalks and talking with their neighbors; everything looked so neat and trim and neighborly that we decided to go back down to the three houses that were still for sale. It was almost dark when we walked up to the largest house, but the lights were on inside it. I wasn't interested in any of them, but Val insisted that we look at this one. I was peeking in the windows, but Jeff naturally pushed the door open, and suddenly he and Val dashed into the house followed by Joanna. I was still lingering outside, and then Jeff zipped back out and grabbed my hand and said, "Come on, dad, you have to see this". He was still on the run and was still on the go as I finished my story in December 2024, although he had slowed down a little when he was fifty-five, but barely so. I was totally shocked when I saw the inside. Everything was so beautiful and well designed. It had almost thirteen hundred square feet on each floor: basement, ground floor, top floor, and attic.

We found business cards for the builder and the realtor. Chris Hamby was the builder and was a super nice man who went to the same church that I did when I was saved at the age of twenty-five. I pulled my cell phone out, and he immediately recognized my voice. I told him that we were looking at the house and was ready to pay cash but did not want to pay the realtor fee. He said that the real estate agent had not done anything for a long time, so he terminated his agreement, and we gave him a check the same night. We started furniture shopping the following morning and had moved in shortly before a lawyer completed the contract.

I went into the office building where the president, vice presidents, and directors' offices were located, and mine was supposed to be, but President Bob O advised me that the USAF colonel who was the military officer in charge of the factory had seen it and moved into it. Bob O located an even larger office, and it was already fully equipped including a secretary. He and I were the only two people who had a private secretary. VP Davy Crockett had undergone quadruple heart bypass surgery and retired. VP Charley R had replaced him. It was my job to write a letter to each of the Hercules operators and have my secretary type a flawless letter, then Tom C would nitpick it. He was a born nitpicker who would spend hours searching for flaws, then he would hold the paper to a light and look for creases or an indication of paper flaws. The only problem I could see was my secretary's typewriter; it was a simple electric typewriter with no smart features, so if my secretary made a minor mistake, she would have to destroy the page and start over because corrections were prohibited. It took me less than four hours to write the letters and ten days for my secretary to produce sixty-five flawless letters and envelopes. It took Tom C almost the same time to admit that they passed his critique. The president signed each of them, and they were mailed. I read each of the responses as they came in and discussed these at Charlie R's staff meetings. Only a few owners/operators replied, and they were in unison: 1. Why does it take so long to get a quote for spare parts? 2. Why is the cost so high? I knew the answers, but it took several months to get people to admit it. Overhead costs are easy to understand and difficult to reduce. First, an aircraft manufacturing company should not have unnecessary tiers of management. Out-of-control vendor prices will sometimes cause the aircraft manufacturer to lose sales. Labor unions drive the cost of all products by insisting on more money for employees, and the cost of goods increase; therefore, the employees' real income is less. The only winners are the mafia lords who own the unions! Bob O's good intentions were in vain. We had spent three years flogging a dead horse. We still had the same two problems that we had in the beginning of Customer Feedback and Evaluation.

A new good deal had just been dreamed up to overjoy me. The governor of New York had called the president of Lockheed Corporation, who called the president of Lockheed Georgia, who then tapped the fall guy (me) for the job. The governor of New York apparently had given all of the money to American-hating illegal aliens and now expected some redneck rebel to pull his rear end out of the fire: translation to say that he expected Lockheed Georgia to spend countless millions of dollars to set up and operate a commercial aircraft repair/overhaul center in upstate in the New York Rochester area where only a lost pilot would land. Tom had always been a true company man with a no-nonsense attitude, so it was a pleasure to travel with him. We landed at LaGuardia Airport NYC, and I rented a car for the drive to Rochester. We checked into our hotel and rested a

Lockheed Employment – 1981-1990

couple of hours before going for a short walk to have a "not too bad dinner". An entourage of people met us in the lobby the next morning. A young man from the governor's office began the presentations in the conference room at nine AM on the dot, followed by the commander of the area highway patrol, and all of the interested civics clubs added to the reasons they wanted to have an aircraft repair/overhaul facility. Of course, the primary purpose was to have jobs available. The AFB had closed, and all jobs disappeared; therefore, the tax-paying working-class citizens moved to areas that had jobs for them. The area needed new taxpayers to support the spending habits of left-wing politicians, thus proving my suppositions before we came up there. Tom and I collected their documents, videos, etc.. We thanked each person and promised that we would make our recommendations to our management. All of us had fake smiles as we shook hands and bid farewell. They were ready to report that they had hooked rebel money to bail them out, and I was thinking, "In a pig's eye will any of our money move up there!" Tom was simply thinking. I explained what he should think on the way back to Atlanta. After I put all of the data and conclusions together and made my presentation, Tom spoke twice as long to close out our/his report. Then Bob O said that Lockheed would not send anything to New York, then commended Tom for a good report. Tom was always modest. Bob thanked me for going with Tom.

Shortly after that, Tom advised me that he had volunteered me for vice president of the Society of Logistics Engineers. Instead of being ecstatic, I was insulted. How could a person who knows a little about packing and shipping claim to be an engineer? He was avid about this new program and had sold Lockheed top officials into letting him create a new department called "Logistics," so we were head-to-head for the first time, especially when he expected me to host a meeting at Lockheed in about four months. It got worse when he insisted that I take the managers of customer services, customer support, customer supply, and logistics to Boston, Massachusetts, ten days later to help them host a meeting. It so happened that upper management officials were having a party the following Friday night and insisted that I attend. Bob R, VP for C-130/L-100 Hercules Programs, was among a group who were chatting about logistics when Bob commented that he was happy to share that I was vice president of the Society of Logistics Engineers. Everyone except me was pleased.

Shortly afterwards, several dignitaries from foreign countries were coming to Lockheed, and in view of the fact I was their primary contact, I was invited to attend a party that was being hosted by the president and vice presidents. I hemmed Bob R in a corner and told him that I was looking for a way out of my present position. He offered me a job that would make me directly under him as director of manufacturing. That meant that about three hundred hourly employees would be working for me, and I would have to contend with the union, so I just got quiet. He knew how I felt, so he said that he was sorry, but he would get everyone involved. I was immediately sorry that I had broached the subject, but it was already set for me to regret it even more. I spent all of the weekend in prayer because knew that the president, vice presidents, and directors would be hurt

Lockheed Employment – 1981-1990

because they were already looking for a good position for me, and I was impatient. I had already declined the job as managing director of operations in Saudi Arabia twice, so the young man Tom (?), whom I had met in Tripoli, Libya, was being interviewed. Lockheed had approximately eleven hundred people in the country, so he could earn a lot of money, but not many who were qualified would accept the offer. Tom was currently the manager of field service operations in North America. I had a long conversation with Tom after which he went to Saudi Arabia, and I accepted his job.

Bob R, Karl K, Davy Crockett, and others have said the same thing my teachers and professors had drummed into me: "You have a good and inquisitive brain and seem to live for challenges, but that can be dangerous because there will be times when there are no challenges, so you must be prepared to deal with that". Easy to say, but I got so bored that I had trouble dealing with it. Sharing God's word with unbelievers was always a challenge, but also a blessing. I believe that's why HE gave the ability to teach His Word to so many people around the world. Then I was fifty years old and needed five more years with Lockheed Martin in order to qualify for early retirement (at some time the two companies merged, and I must remember that the junior partner's name should be added). I had a job and had to keep on keeping on until after May 1989. I had to travel all over the forty-eight continental states plus Alaska. I had been to Hawaii twice even though no C-130 aircraft were based there. The USAF, the Navy, Marines, Coast Guard, Air National Guard, and Air Force Reserves had bases throughout the USA. A few still had Lockheed reps under contract, but most units had to rely on the generosity of Lockheed Martin, Georgia, to solve a few problems. We provided free service by field service reps who were based at designated locations and then rotate around all regions of his area. I made trips to Alaska and throughout the forty-eight continental states every year for four years.

Then in 1988, President Bob O and two vice presidents went to Cambridge, England, to see Sir Arthur Marshall, and he recalled that Bill Walls had moved back to the USA for six years so his children could retain their US citizenship. The six years were up, so could you persuade him to come back here? Bob agreed to try to talk me into it. When the question was presented to me, I did not really know what to say, because I knew that Val was still in love with Pakistan. I knew that I had to mention it, so she said, "Of course, you did say yes, I will go back to England". She was ready to start packing and selling, but I didn't really want to go, and Joanna did not want to go. Jeffry said he would like to go. That really put me in a quandary because we split again on what we wanted to do. Jeffry had just finished high school and was ready for the first year of college, and he had already been enrolled. Val insisted that Jeff get into the college, as it would be better for him to see what it was like to be on his own, and I did not want that. I wanted him with me too. Joanna had a crush on a little boy in the first year of high school, and she did not want to go to England, but I lost the battle. I flew to England and arranged to rent the same house that we had lived in several years earlier. Val, Jeffry, and Jo were packing, so we put the house on the market. We put the furniture and clothing in a climate-controlled warehouse and enrolled Jeff in Kennesaw College. Valerie was the only

Lockheed Employment – 1981-1990

happy person in the family. She was getting out of the USA, Jo and I were leaving the country we loved, and Jeff was on his own for the first time in his life.

In the meantime, Press H, the new C-130 sales representative for Africa, called and asked me if I could get him an appointment in Morocco. No one had been able to get into headquarters. I said, "No problem". I promised to meet him in Rabat three days later. A hurricane was headed toward the United States, and then all of a sudden it turned around and headed to Europe. Everyone in Europe thought that was funny because no one had ever heard of a hurricane hitting England. We arrived safely at London's Heathrow Airport and took a large taxi all the way up to Cambridge and moved into our old house. Then the wind picked up fast and howled throughout the night. We lost power, and the telephones weren't working. Power came on about four in the morning, so I could see how to complete packing of my suitcase. As I walked downstairs, Val and Jo woke up and joined me for a quick breakfast. They knew that I needed to catch my flight to Morocco, but after watching the news on the TV, it seemed impossible because the hurricane had blown trees across railway tracks and the highways. Power lines were down everywhere, although the power was back on in our area. Val and Jo didn't believe that it would be possible to get to the airport, but I had prayed and left it in God's hands; with Him, all things are possible.

I was able to get a taxi to the train station in Cambridge, but the train to London was delayed. I was getting very edgy because the clock was ticking closer to the no-go hour. It finally came into sight at a crawl. Someone hanging out the front was watching for power lines, trees, or other objects on the rails. It finally pulled up to the platform, and I rushed aboard. We arrived at the next station where we were told that was as far as the train could go, so we had to wait for a bus to take us to London. The really bad news was that there was no idea when or if the bus would arrive. Everyone had been told not to get out of their homes because of the utter destruction caused by a hurricane that would never hit the Island of Great Britain. Haha! But I saw no humor. It appeared that I would not even get home, but I would not despair. I was in God's hands. A taxi had pulled up, and several people had forgotten about keeping their stiff upper lips and were fighting to get in. A huge Indian Sikh was literally tossing the people out and said, "Airport only". I rushed over and was thinking about giving him a hug, but fortunately for me, I decided against it. He asked for my flight number, and after I told him, he said that we must hurry. I told him that I would double the meter reading if he made it on time. He told me to buckle up and not distract him by chattering. I was paralyzed by his speed and zigzagging, so I closed my eyes and prayed. We arrived with time to spare, and he was paid double plus a bonus.

I arrived in Rabat, and Press H was in the hotel on schedule. After chatting for a few minutes, I told Press that I would call to arrange appointments for tomorrow. I decided to call the military commander first and received a notice that the phone was not in service. That set off a warning signal in my head, but I decided to call my other friend, the minister of defense. A voice asked who was calling, and I gave him a pre-arranged code name to protect both of us in the event there was a problem. There was always that possibility in

Lockheed Employment – 1981-1990

Morocco because there had been three attempts to assassinate the king since I had met my two friends. The stranger spoke to someone and then told me that the minister does not accept calls at home, "so you must go to his office at ten tomorrow and ask for an appointment". I thanked him for his information, then signaled Press H to keep quiet and follow me. We walked down the sidewalk to a nice quiet restaurant as I explained in a low voice that something had happened. I didn't know what, but we would have an appointment tomorrow at ten. We enjoyed our Moroccan dinner followed by a good sleep. We arrived at the minister's office fifteen minutes before our scheduled meeting and were kept waiting by his secretary until precisely ten AM. The minister opened the door and asked us to come in. He left the door open, thus convincing me that something was amiss. We shook hands, and I introduced Press. He told us that he appreciated the technical support, but there was nothing in their budget for new aircraft at the moment. He had asked General Mohamed, the military commander, to come to his office and show us around. We were introduced to the general, and then he ushered us out, but gently slowed me down to say goodbye to me and assure me that he was OK. We had a strong handshake and parted forever. Press and I had a short conversation with the general and drove to the air base where we spent about three hours with the C-130 troops. I knew that this would be my last opportunity to visit because I planned to retire, so I gave them a fond farewell. When I arrived in Cambridge, most of the evidence of the hurricane had disappeared. I rented another car and spent a week with Sir Arthur and all of his personnel at Marshall

Aerospace. Everyone seemed happy to have me back, and Sir Arthur was much more than "happy".

I visited all of the countries in Europe, and one day Don Braham, Manager of Customer Service and Training, called to tell me that Lockheed had sold two L-100 Hercules to Angola. A Field Service Representative was included in the contract, so someone from management would have to go to Angola to assess the situation before a rep could go, and he "wondered if I would be willing to do that". I should have done a little thinking about the destruction that Peanut President Jimmy Carter had done to Africa before telling Don that I would be pleased to go. There was more to this than I could have imagined. The USA did not have an Embassy or any relationship with Angola. If I had a problem in the country, I would have to try to locate the Italian Charge d'Affaires (assuming there was one and assuming he was alive and not in prison) and assuming he liked rednecks from Georgia and would be overjoyed to attempt to get me out of prison. I always thought that I was brave, but this was suicidal. I was about to discover that this was an understatement.

I packed two suitcases and flew to Lisbon, Portugal, to meet officials of Angola National Airlines because they owned the Hercules and could get a visa for me. Angola was controlled by Russia, so it was impossible to get a visa outside Angola. A Lockheed Sales Representative who was married to a Caucasian Angolan woman just happened to be in my hotel in Lisbon to ensure that things would go well for my trip. They portrayed Angola as an island paradise, when it was neither. I bought a first-class ticket on the Portuguese airline

Lockheed Employment – 1981-1990

TAP, and the only good thing about the service was the lack of it. At least I made it safely to Luanda, the capital city of Angola. The airport might have looked good before Democrat Jimmy Carter decided that he would "change the country". It now looked like a rundown saloon in the old western movies. I needed a couple of .45 revolvers on my hips now. Nobody looked like me, and I didn't see a friendly face. I certainly didn't see a visa for me. I moved through customs without a problem, but then got into a single line leading to a desk with an evil-looking man seated behind it. Looks are sometimes deceiving, but not so here. I was struggling with my suitcases and slowly heading towards the firing squad. There were about five men in the room armed with Uzi submachine guns. The men were not Angolan or Russians, so that left Cubans. The Russians had been using Cubans in their efforts to overthrow the peaceful government, and the CIA were resisting them when Jimmy Carter got on his white horse and told the rightful leaders to surrender.

I finally got to the desk and handed my passport to the nice man and said, "Good Evening, sir". He was busy thumbing through my passport, then stuck my passport up in my face and shouting some weird things. If you are in a situation like that, you better understand that he wants to see a visa. I tried a few words of Indonesian mixed with Spanish mixed with pig Latin and South Georgia y'alls, but somehow he had a little problem with languages and couldn't comprehend that I was trying to explain that his airline office had my visa and even pointed to their office, which was next door. Usually, foreigners can understand better if you shout louder, but he canceled my theory by throwing my passport under his desk and pointing to the door. He shouted, "Go!" I cheered up because he seemed like a good old boy with a sense of humor because he spoke English. I knew that he understood me when I politely told him that I could not leave without my passport. Wrong again. He set off an alarm by touching a switch. A large army rushed in through the doors with guns zeroed on me. I put both hands and one foot up in the air but quickly got the message that I needed to pick up my cases and evacuate. I illegally walked up the ramp to the airline office to portray an angry American. I was set aback by everyone's greeting; "Mr. Walls, it's wonderful to see you. We sent your visas to the office in Lisbon, and we are surprised that you are here so quickly". I told them of my harassment and loss of my passport. They were so sorry, but assured (or tried to) that my passport would be returned soon. I was introduced to two Englishmen and were told that they would spend full time showing me around the city. There were no privately owned houses, cars, hotels, restaurants, or anything. I commented about the decay of living conditions and life in general since the government had been replaced, but was told that my comment was very dangerous. For the first time in my life, someone changed my attitude (just for now). I was given the key to my room in a seventeen-story hotel with the restaurant on top. The Englishmen (for clarification I'll call them Roy and Roy) drove to the hotel and parked the car. They helped carry my luggage inside where I had to check in. The cost was two hundred dollars cash per night, and the meals were extra. All was free if I worked for the government. I knew I was being gouged but was still keeping my opinions to myself for health's sake. I had to pay two thousand dollars up front. I

Lockheed Employment – 1981-1990

advised the clerk that I expected to eat at other restaurants most of the time, but he was too happy to inform me that there weren't any other restaurants. It was almost time for dinner, so we dropped my bags in my room. They washed up in their room while I did the same in my bathroom, and we met at the elevator. A single lane had already formed there waiting to charge in and take a seat where waiters would deliver a plate of food (?) and a glass of someone's body temperature of water to each person. Of course, the waiter dropped the utensils somewhere in the area. Everything probably had been clean before President Carter had demanded that Portuguese settlers leave Angola and let communist Russia relieve the country of its evil diamonds and other precious jewels. Now I had an up-close and personal view of the way the people prospered. Time to give credit where credit is due and dishonor where it is due! Thank the Lord for my cast iron stomach and intestines!

After a restless night of considering the events thus far, I had another blah meal, and tears came into my eyes as I realized that many local people would work most of the day for a portion of what I planned to trash; I picked up my fork and cleaned my plate. Roy and Roy thought I was thoughtful about not wasting food. We visited our rooms for an hour to take care of the necessities before starting our day touring. City buses were the only vehicles other than the car we were riding in, and they were totally overfilled. The few cars and other methods of transportation were assigned to government offices. Any person could use the buses, but the only places that ordinary citizens needed transportation to was their homes, workplace, or the food warehouse. Workers never received money but just a piece of paper showing the amount of money he had earned, and this could only be redeemed at the government warehouse. I questioned the reason there were no women in sight, and I was told that women had no right to work; they had to depend on their husbands for food. If her supplier died or kicked her out, she had to work in a special building where other men would visit and pay a little for the favors she showed. If she became popular, she might live a few more years. The government confiscated all children of the poor at birth and did whatever they wished with the infants, because big brother owned "Everything and everybody". Radicals in the free country USA are working to put Russia in control of America the same as Jimmy Carter, Ted Turner, George Soros, Bill Gates, Joe Biden, and others I could name have done and are still working on. The climate change imbeciles are trying to use a made-up claim to control us, similar to the man-made covid that fooled a few people. (More on the one-world government conspiracies later.)

I needed to see what medical support would be available, so we went to the hospital. The small hospital and staff were very helpful. I was favorably impressed for the first time since arriving there. We drove around the outer area of the city to a large prison, or so the Roys said. A sign confirmed it, but there were no outer walls, fences, guard towers, guards, or other usual things, just a sign: PRISON. I'm sure it had a welcome mat, but I felt no need to verify it. This was the prison where the captured CIA agents were being left to die after Jimmy Carter invited the Russians to put their man in power, and thus take over the second largest mines in the world of diamonds, other precious metals, plus oil, etc. We drove a couple of miles out a two-lane road and came to a

Lockheed Employment – 1981-1990

road block with all kinds of warning signs. This was to prevent anyone from entering or leaving the jungle a short distance ahead. Supposedly, some CIA operatives were trapped in the jungle. They would kill anyone entering, and the Cubans or Russians would kill anyone leaving it. The jail behind us held the operatives that were captured when Carter told the conservative government to step down. The Cubans were doing close-up support of the leftist government that had taken over, and the Russians had a large army and Air Force there for total control. They also had "advisors" embedded in the Angola government. Good deal for our arch-enemy, if what I had seen and heard was true, and it had to be true. I had all of the information in my head that I needed (it would probably give me a fatal dose of Sudden Death Syndrome if it were in writing). It is still in my head about forty years later as I am writing my memoirs. In fact, I still have a vivid knowledge of all events I have witnessed since I was six years old. Unbelievable, probably, but True and very scary. Why me?

When we returned to the zero-star hotel, someone from Angola Airlines walked up and handed me my passport with a visa very clearly stamped in it. He told me that my first-class seat on the Portuguese Air flight to Lisbon at ten AM tomorrow was confirmed. He hoped, without meaning it, that I would come back. I said what I meant: "Ain't NO WAY!" "NEVER" was added as a confirmation. Roy and Roy drove me to the airport, and as we were saying goodbye, I slipped them a few hundred green back bills that Angola Air would refund. I ducked under their grateful kisses to my cheeks. I wanted to remember them as good old boys. Doubtful for sure, but I had to hope for the best.

At this time in 2024 that I am writing, Joe Biden made a trip to Angola, returned to DC, and went on TV to announce that he was sending a tremendous amount of taxpayer's money as aid to Angola. In my humble opinion, this would prove beneficial to his retirement. After all, he no longer has the illegally obtained secret documents; therefore, the Biden Cartel can no longer receive an unknown millions of dollars from China. Bless his heart, he might have dementia so badly that he has no knowledge of his surroundings because he has learned how to make big bucks as a dealer with foreign enemies. (I can justify spreading the truth about him because I have been dealing with Alzheimer's for at least three years, which is longer than he has, but I am a patriot, and that makes a big difference about how a person looks at money.) Regardless, Biden's donation will provide the money that Russia needs to harvest the Angola diamonds and other precious jewels, titanium, and oil. Surely the puppet master would toss his trusty puppet at least a few billion dollars for his cause. Just proves that if you own a jackass, you have to feed him. That is a good analogy, even if I do say so.

Just for a moment, let's take a look at what is being revealed and most people know: "The Russians are using slave labor to mine the diamonds and other jewels, but can only slip a few out at a time without sharing them with the puppet government". "They are running out of time to destroy the USA with nuclear bombs before Trump is sworn in". "If they could just find a way to convince Biden to make a surprise visit in Air Force One and load a trillion dollars worth of jewels which he could pay for with one billion dollars of US 'Aid'". That would be adequate for Russia to finish equipping its supersonic ballistic missiles with atomic warheads and

Lockheed Employment – 1981-1990

join China, North Korea, and Iran in a surprise nuclear attack to destroy all of North America. Impossible? It can happen and will happen very soon. That is why North America is not mentioned in the Book of Revelation. The time is running out for non-believers to get right with Jesus Christ. It will soon be too late!

When I got home and was preparing to write my report, Val walked in to notify me that she was filing for divorce. When I was down, I was now being figuratively kicked. I knew it would happen someday, and I could not change her mind, so I agreed to a non-protested divorce; otherwise, a couple of lawyers would end up with all of our money. It would be better for her to have what she wanted, and I would have the rest for Jo and Jeff. Ricky was married and would soon open his medical practice. I could not blame Val because we never should have married. It's always the children who suffer the most, although my heart was broken because my family was broken. That is another thing I would have to deal with.

I continued with my report, wherein I listed the hazards, lack of food and drinking water, etc.. I suggested that the field service rep receive a fifty percent increase in pay for "war zone" conditions and that it should be mandatory that he leave his wife in the USA. Everyone agreed, but the rep defied orders and took his wife with him. I was told that both of them developed severe intestine problems where amoeba consumes every object. He recovered, but his wife lost the battle. I understand that he was a "semper fi" marine, but never asked whether he showed remorse for taking his wife with him.

When Jo got out of King's College school in Ely for the summer break, we flew back to Georgia where Val received the divorce. Ricky had completed five years at Emory University and four years at the University of Georgia Medical College with a PhD for oral and maxillofacial surgery. He and Julie had purchased a small house, and Julie taught high school math while Ricky was getting his soon-to-become a very successful practice. I stayed with them for two weeks before returning to Cambridge. I spent most of the time at Marshall of Cambridge until Joanna returned in July for enrollment for the last year of school before going to college. She and I decided it would be more prudent if she were a boarder in the girl's dorm. She had asked me to buy a Renault for her sixteenth birthday a year before, so I kept her loaded with money. I moved into a hotel a little closer to Ely and lived there, except when I was traveling to Turkey and all countries in Europe to advise my friends that I planned to retire the following March, but would be back soon thereafter. All of them hated to see me go but were pleased to know that I would return. The thing I dreaded most was having to say farewell to Sir Arthur and his staff. He gave me a wonderful retirement party and another solid silver Armada Dish with his emblem in it. I spent an entire day shaking hands with everyone.

The next morning, which was about the middle of March 1990, I called Lockheed to state that I had enough and was going to retire. Everyone wanted to know why, and would I please reconsider or accept another position anywhere, but please don't retire now because I was so young. I reminded the officials that I had warned them that I was tired of doing things that others either could not do or didn't want to do, so

Lockheed Employment – 1981-1990

it was too late to make amends or promise to do better. "So sorry. Good bye". I closed my accounts and sold my Lockheed stock, etc., much to my chagrin. The stock would be worth several million dollars now. My short temper cost me very dearly. I still receive monthly retirement checks, but they would be almost triple the amount if I had waited ten years and three months for normal retirement. Not time to consider what could have been. After my divorce, I couldn't face my friends and reply to their questions of "WHY?" I took my money and left, which was a terrible decision.

Chapter 11
Marketing & Conclusions - 1990-2025

The word spread throughout the industry that I was retiring, and everyone knew of my contacts. Two companies that sold components and accessories for the C-130 Hercules asked me to work for them. One was in England and the other in Wisconsin. I refused to discuss it before cutting ties with Lockheed because I would have a conflict of interest. Two weeks before my chosen retirement date, I visited my friend, Attorney Duard McDonald, a Christian and conservative politician. He was a relative of Larry McDonald, leader of the John Birch Society. That society helped search for communists who had infiltrated our society: education, politics, and many other groups. Senator John McCarthy had already identified government officials, college professors, FBI officials, and many others, and they were being investigated and charged as spies. That made Larry and the senator targets of China, Russia, and the spies in the USA.

Larry McDonald was a passenger on a commercial flight from the U.S. to the Far East for a business meeting with officials who were also concerned about the penetration of communism in their countries. The commercial aircraft was in free airspace over the Atlantic Ocean when North Korea shot it down with a rocket, killing Larry and everyone else on board. The reason for this was suppressed by liberal news and politicians controlled by the mega-rich. The entrenched spies in America and other nations had eliminated their

problem, except for Senator McCarthy. He had already been declared a radical because he loved his country. He was removed from his Senate position and lost his seat during the next election because the mega-rich had used their television and radio stations to spread lies about him and the John Birch Society. The John Birchers were destroyed, and the communists then had a free hand to work on plans for a one-world government with total control. I had formed a relationship with the John Birch Society while in college because I also loved the USA. Now my ties were broken, and I thought I might be wise by keeping quiet. Sometime in the near future, I'll write an exposé on conspiracies and how all of them are intertwined. It's satanic, believe it or not!

Now, back to Attorney McDonald. He had sold his law firm, including the multi-story office building, to his associates. He currently rented a suite in a bank building, and his wife was the secretary. All of us loved golf but had never played together. At that moment, I was setting up an "S" Corporation for International Aircraft Marketing Consultancy Limited to protect me from legal damages if the company was sued. On the last day of March 1990, I left Lockheed Martin Corporation for early retirement. Lockheed had purchased Northrop Aviation, an electronics company, a shipbuilding company, and merged with Martin Rocket and Space Company. Martin was a relatively small company, but managers from all the companies had commingled, leaving no camaraderie.

I had a contract ready to accept a marketing advisor position with a C-130 component sales company. I ignored the offers from England and Wisconsin and contacted X company in

Fort Lauderdale, Florida. They were eager to see me and said they would refund my money if I purchased a ticket. I flew into Fort Lauderdale and rented a car for the short trip to the office. The two owners, Deano and Donk, took me out for lunch and wanted to know what I expected to receive to handle their marketing. I said that I would take the job if they would pay me $700/week for travel expenses plus one percent commission on all increased sales, and I would spend a few months contacting all of the European C-130 operators and service companies. They replied with an offer of one percent of all sales, including the current fourteen million annual sales the company currently had, but I would have to bear the very high cost of international travel. I said that was risky but agreed. We went to their office to sign the contract with my corporation so that my commission would be paid into my corporate account. They signed it and then insisted that they sign an agreement stating that I would receive one percent of all sales of components and component overhaul. After that, they introduced me to the manager of sales, Roger M., who was very unhappy that I was going to be paid the same amount he was receiving. He was silenced, though. The next employee in the sales department was Roco D'ago. He had met me before and considered me Mr. Lockheed. He was surprised to hear that I wanted to work for a small company after the position I had with Lockheed but told the owners that they were fortunate to have me join them. There were only two others in the sales department. They had a computer specialist, two in the packing and shipping department, and six in the overhaul shops. They also had a receptionist, one secretary for them, and a clerk typist to support the sales, overhaul, and shipping departments. It was a low-budget but efficient setup. The owners knew how to operate a productive and cost-effective company.

I spent a few days with Jeff, Ricky, and Julie and also saw my mother, who was in a nursing home with Alzheimer's. After that, I flew to London and rented a car at Heathrow Airport, driving to Plymouth University to check on Joanna. As a nursing major, she was always in need of more money in her bank account. Then I drove to Cambridge and checked into a hotel. The following morning, I met with Sir Arthur Marshall and Peter Hedderwick. Sir Arthur was walking out the gate to Marshall Aerospace as I walked in. He said, "Is that Bill Walls?" and met me in the middle of the street. He gave me a firm handshake and asked about my family and what I was doing after retirement. He was about ninety-three and almost blind, and Lady Marshall had died. Being a gentleman and friend, he was concerned about me and my family. It just broke my heart! I had a short conversation with Peter, who asked me how things were going. I explained that I now worked for X company and how I could move all the required C-130 overhaul components and parts to his facility. When his technicians used an item, we would send another to restock his supply, and then he would send us money to pay for the unit that Marshall had used. As soon as possible, his people would ship the defective component to X for overhaul. This was a win-win situation for Marshall Aerospace, so he didn't hesitate to sign an agreement. I worked out a similar arrangement for most of the operators in Europe and then flew back to Fort Lauderdale. Several foreign embassies in Washington, D.C., had an Air Force

Marketing & Conclusions – 1990-2025

officer to purchase aircraft components, so I spent a week visiting applicable offices and securing their business.

In 1992, Donk told me that they had always wanted an agreement with Lockheed that would allow X to purchase components from vendors at the same price that Lockheed paid. They had not been able to see anyone except Friendly Fox, who was their contact when they wanted to purchase an item. Donk had nothing more to offer but thought my contacts would be enough to work. My best contacts had died or retired, but I called John C., who had replaced Tom C. as Director of Product Support and Logistics. I knew that he had been with one of the other companies that Lockheed had purchased, and he didn't fit in (like trying to put a square stick into a round hole), so someone had unloaded him to replace Tom when he retired. Tom's secretary was still there and told him that I was asking for an appointment. He remembered me and that I had connections over his head, so I had an appointment with him the following morning at nine. I was greeted with a big hug by the secretary, and we talked for several minutes before the subject of my appointment came up, and she finally told me to go in. John was scrambling around, trying to look busy. After shaking hands, he asked what he could do for me, and I replied that we would like to find a way for us to help each other. Lockheed had paid hundreds of companies around the world to develop parts and components for the C-130 aircraft, and those companies had signed an agreement not to sell those items to anyone except Lockheed or the U.S. government. John didn't see anything wrong with that picture and was about to boot me out when "Bill Walls!" rang out from the doorway. It was Terry G., whom I met when I was the C-130

Program Manager in Tehran, and he arrived as the assistant to the P-3 Program Manager. He was now the Executive Vice President of Lockheed Martin (I almost forgot to add Martin). He asked how things were going with me and what I was doing now. I told him that I was trying to work out a teaming agreement between company X and Lockheed Martin so we could take some business away from company Y in Wisconsin. He asked whether I thought we could do that, and I told him that it would work. He noticed John and said, "Bill Walls knows more about the C-130 than anyone in the world; do what he tells you to do". He told me to let him know if he could help me. We hugged, and he was gone. John suddenly decided that he wanted to get started right away.

I called Donk and Roger, but neither wanted to believe that I had accomplished what they believed impossible. I told them of my discussions with John and me about how my friend, Executive Vice President Terry G., had interceded to give us the teaming agreement. I told them that I would be there to introduce them to everyone involved if they wanted to have an agreement; otherwise, they could just forget it forever. They caught the first flight to Atlanta and checked into the Sheraton Hotel where I was staying. They were still in disbelief. The following morning, I introduced them to John C. and then to Matt H., Manager of Supply. John would be busy, so he told Matt to follow my lead. Matt and his supervisors made notes, and by the end of the day, we had a basic agreement with the promise that the contracts department would have a contract in a few days. On the way out, we bumped into Friendly Fox, who was so happy to see all three of us and was elated when Donk and Roger advised

Marketing & Conclusions – 1990-2025

of how their "efforts" had paid off; now they had a teaming agreement. Foxy thought briefly and suddenly recalled that he had worked behind the scenes to put it in motion. Donk and Roger decided to stay another night to celebrate with Foxy the great things they had done. Foxy called Matt to get a short vacation so he could fly at X's expense to Fort Lauderdale to make a joint announcement to the X peasants. It was enough to make a buzzard regurgitate, but no one even noticed when I walked out the door. I spent a few days with Jeff, Ricky, and Julie and visited my mother in the nursing home. The sad thing was her Alzheimer's was so advanced that she didn't look at anything but the ceiling. She died and went home to be with her Lord Jesus Christ in 1994. After that, she had a Heavenly body with no more suffering.

Roco and I continued to attend all four major air shows in London, Paris, Dubai, and Singapore. One year I went alone to the show in Santiago, Chile, South America; however, I did not meet a single prospective customer. I had wasted a ton of my money on a trip that Donk had requested I make. Never again. One year we were in our booth at the Dubai Air Show, and a large group of Filipino men walked up and said, "I bet you don't remember us". I confessed that they were right, and they proudly announced that they followed my darts team in Iran and saw me win two consecutive Iranian championships. I was sad to say goodbye because Filipinos are so humble and nice. At the end of the show, I told Roco that for the first time in my life, I was a bit concerned about my trip to Yemen on the way home. I was never scared anywhere because I was in God's care.

Anyway, I stopped in Egypt to see the pyramids and watch crocodiles climb out of the Nile River and chase the natives up the streets of Cairo. I had a personal guide who spent a lot of time discussing the pyramids. We had many debates about how the Israelis built them. I wrote a paper on the subject in college, and no one could dispute it at that time. I saw an article in a science journal a few years later that had exactly the same conclusion. I don't believe that someone plagiarized me. I never saw the crocodiles chase anyone, so I finally decided to continue to Sana'a, the northern capital of Yemen. The southern section's capital is Aden. It seems that the country is almost always in a civil war because the south is radical Shi'ite Muslim, and the north is moderate Sunni. This was my first time visiting.

As I was checking into the hotel, a man in a dark business suit with a bow tie and a briefcase was walking toward me and saying, "Bill Walls, what a surprise to see you". I was much more surprised than he was. Without a doubt, he was a wealthy British banker, but what did that have to do with me? He saw that I did not recognize him, so he surprised me again. He said that he and I were seated together in first class on a British Air direct flight from London to Tehran. He had purchased a box of expensive Cuban cigars at the duty-free shop at Heathrow Airport and offered one to me, but I declined. Then we were notified that the Tehran airport roof had collapsed and killed numerous people, so we had to stay on board to Kuwait. Although I wasn't a smoker, I enjoyed one of the cigars. We landed in Kuwait only to find that all hotels were overbooked, and all flights out were booked for the next two weeks. Our aircraft was refueled with us on board (Oops. That is taboo). We were only bothered when

Marketing & Conclusions – 1990-2025

the hostess told us to extinguish our cigars until fueling was completed. I was surprised that the fire safety regulations were being enforced (a teeny-weeny bit). As we taxied, the pilot announced the flight time to New Delhi is...!! I asked my latest buddy for another cigar. We landed in New Delhi but parked on the ramp, and my built-in alarms were very loud. The pilot announced that we would not believe this, but the airport had closed because of a cholera epidemic, so the Tehran passengers would have to deplane right here and board the Pan American Airlines plane a few feet away. Might as well toss the safety regulations manual. At least we were finally headed for our destination if someone could remember where it was. No one bothered to mention that the next stop was Bahrain, where Tehran passengers and baggage were kicked off. Even a Christian sometimes gets perturbed. The Lord had spent a lot of time trying to teach me to be patient, and I prayed that He would not continue the training, so I zipped my lips and waited for the hammer to fall again. Finally, a small, over-used, outdated puddle jumper plane took us to Tehran because a new path had been created through the airport. I knew that my chauffeur would be there to pick me up, but all of my detours had kept him jumping for twenty-eight hours. He showed up as I was about to leave in a taxi. Val and the kids had been watching TV and were almost certain that I had arrived. That saga happened a few years ago, so back to the present.

I already knew that the Yemen Air Force bought everything from Y, so I hoped to change that. Deano had approved a four hundred thousand dollar letter of credit just in case I could use that to bargain. About eight officers were seated around the room and telling me that if they purchased a component from us, they would check it for a while and take more than a month to pay for it. I told them that I couldn't understand why they were going through all of that when I was offering them a four-hundred-thousand-dollar bill of credit. They moved faster than a football team, sitting up and looking at one another, then a general asked me to repeat what I said, which I did. He said that he wanted the Air Force commander to hear that. While he was gone, someone explained that the commander was the president's brother. The commander was so impressed that we received all of their requirements and would receive orders for all items that were previously purchased from Y company, usually a million dollars per year. Lockheed had moved close to a hundred million dollars worth of high-value items to X and paid X fifteen percent of the value per year to store the items. X could sell them and pay Lockheed the Lockheed cost, which was a fantastic deal for X. X could now purchase components from the vendors at the same price Lockheed paid. In addition, an inspector was moved down to certify the overhauled components, which would increase the value. X was making so much money in 1996 that Donk told me that I had more money than I could spend, so I should retire and smell the roses, but I advised him that I did not have enough money to retire. Roger convinced Donk to hire a young Marine officer who was in charge of the supply office in a U.S. Marine C-130 Base. I couldn't imagine what he would be able to do because he knew absolutely nothing that would benefit X. That was nothing to concern me, though. Donk was talked into making the guy vice president for marketing, and that was absolutely ludicrous.

Marketing & Conclusions – 1990-2025

In 1998, sales were about forty million dollars, and Donk told me that no one was worth the kind of money that I would earn, so he stopped the commission and would pay me ninety thousand/year. I impolitely told him to stuff it; I was cutting the ties immediately. He was now very pale because he could see the handwriting on the wall and walked into Deano's office. Deano was not aware of the problem his partner had created, but both of them came to my office to apologize and asked me to stay at least until they could sell the company. I said that I would give them a maximum of six months. Deano and I had a long conversation; he and I were best friends and would continue. He had been blindsided, so I enlightened him: My work had increased X's income thirty-five million per year, and Donk was making so much more that he could not afford to pay me the one percent that he insisted on and signed an agreement on in 1990. I asked Deano not to let this destroy his long partnership with Donk. The company was advertised for sale, and several companies started checking their assets to determine whether they could afford to bid. The only two that could afford it were Lockheed Martin and a New York Jew, Max, who had a business partner named Zve. I had talked with them when they asked me to help them compete with X. I explained that I could not double-cross X. Zve agreed with me, but Max became disgusted with me. Now Max had sold his assets to Zve and then borrowed against the future to compete. I decided that it was time to let Terry G. know that I was leaving. When he learned that I had quit, Lockheed dropped out and let Max purchase X. Lockheed pulled the rep and the one hundred million dollars worth of parts back to the factory and broke all ties with X. Lockheed also purchased

Y in Wyoming. Roger and his short-term Marine would be running the new company and were celebrating because Roco and I were calling each way. I let the second axe fall. I spent two days letting my friends around the world know that I was no longer with X, and Lockheed purchased Y, thus Lockheed Martin had ideal sources for providing quality parts at the best prices. Now Max and his new cohorts had parts but no customers. It took much less than a year for their house of cards to collapse and go bankrupt. Such a sad ending.

I rushed through the 1990s, but I went back to mention my visits to see Joanna. She had graduated from Plymouth University with a bachelor's degree as an RN, then worked in a cancer ward. She met Dave Klahn, an architect specializing in the design of hospitals and medical centers. Jeff and I were there for me to walk with her down the aisle for their wedding. I hosted a large wedding party at a hotel where everyone spent the night. The next morning, they left for their honeymoon; Jeff returned to the U.S., and I continued travels to secure more business for X. Jeff and I were back to see Olivia, Alex, and Benjamin after each was born. They moved to Richmond, Virginia, in 2003, where Jo and Dave had jobs waiting for them. Jeff was living in Virginia also but near Washington D.C., where he was running a large air charter business and teaching people how to fly. Now I could drive a relatively short distance to see all of my family three or four times per year. I was as happy as a South Georgia pig in a mud puddle, or so it seemed to me.

I had to stop for a moment to recall that I had no money when I left our farm in 1950 to earn a fortune. After fifty years of hard work, I had almost a tad of money. On the other hand, I had the world's best two sons and a daughter, all of whom were on their way toward fantastic careers, meaning they would have a better life than I. I loved them, and they loved me. That had been my lifelong dream. Who could possibly ask for more? I had a small home with a soon-to-be wonderful wife with food on the table, so I thank God for His Blessings on me. (Slight plagiarization of an Alan Jackson hit song, but maybe he will forgive me because I cannot sing it.) God allowed me to have a short vacation playing golf before giving me another job working for Him. I sold my condo in Fort Lauderdale and bought a nice small house in north Florida, which was five miles from the cattle ranch that my friends Alvin and Edith owned. There were two country clubs in Lake City and several more nearby. Jeff decided to skip college in 1990 and joined the Navy in 1993. He ran the lab at night in the Jacksonville, Florida, naval base hospital for almost six and a half years. He attended Jacksonville College during the day until he received a diploma for a bachelor's degree and later graduated from pilot's training. Alvin had to have chemo and radiation treatments for melanoma cancer about three years after I settled into my intensive golf schedule, so I reduced my golf for one year. Of course, I also attended a local Baptist church with Al and Edith. After the treatments, the melanoma went into remission, and my golf increased for a short time until the associate pastor volunteered me to do a little, a.k.a. a lot, of work at the church.

The Lord let me know that my vacation was over the first of 2010. The church treasurer had left for greener pastures, and the only people left to take care of the finances were three brilliant ladies, neither of whom enjoyed crunching numbers. One of them was Edith's younger sister, who had borrowed my new 1955 Bel Air Sport Coupe a half-century earlier. Anyway, Juanita came up and quietly told me that they needed help and asked me to join the finance team. I considered that to be a sacred job and told her to find someone else, but she said that no one else could do it. I want everyone to pay close attention: "Twenty years ago, I retired from an excellent job with Lockheed Martin and was now being coerced into a non-paying job". Juanita trapped me when she added, "Please, you are our only hope". Women were in distress, so I had to saddle my white horse and ride. It was Bill to the rescue! This appears kind of iffy on paper, but I will stick with it because this was my first and last chance to be a hero. I will try to remember to accidentally work this into conversations the rest of my life. The church bylaws specified that a person must be approved by vote at a business meeting for a two-year term for the hallowed position as treasurer. I was hijacked into it and brought it up in business meetings four times a year for thirteen years before I hired a neurologist to give me a letter stating that I had Alzheimer's and might bite someone.

Edith, Juanita, and I were with Alvin when his doctor notified him that the melanoma had returned with a vengeance and had spread to his brain and other parts of his body, so there was nothing to do. He probably had six months, but somewhat less than a year to live. The primary object the three of us had was to make Al's last days as pleasant as possible. Al and Edith had been hiding plans for my surprise eightieth birthday party for several months. Ricky, Julie, Jeff, and Jo, and my friend Dean, a.k.a. Deano from X, were in on it, as were all of the members of Peace Baptist Church in Branford. The pastor and associate pastor tricked me into taking them to my favorite restaurant in Gainesville, The Indian Cuisine, on Saturday, May 11, 2013. After we left the restaurant, my betrayers realized that we were ahead of schedule, so one of them noticed that my diesel F-250 pickup had less than a half tank of fuel remaining, hoping to slow down the refuel process. Neither of us knew that Jeff was directly behind us when I turned into a service station in Fort White. Jeff zipped past and joined Ricky, Dean, and the rest. Jo was having a knee problem and was unable to attend. My ex-friends asked me to drop them off at the church, but there were more cars in the parking lot than on Easter when the once or twice a year Christians come in for their annual blessing. I had to assume that the ladies were having a special meeting, but I was not going inside. I could not be wrong again, haha. I said my farewells to both Benedict Arnolds; my door opened, and another false friend grabbed my arm and pulled me out the door, saying, "Ya gotta see this". The two radical preachers reaffirmed this as they followed me out the door, and the three of them threw me into the dark fellowship hall. The lights snapped on, and a vicious mob started screaming, "Surprise, Happy Birthday". I was really surprised when I saw Jeff and Ricky move forward. After I had hugged everyone in sight, Dean Stickler walked up and gave me a very firm hug. My Dearest Sister in Christ, Ruth Cornel, took photos and told me that Alvin had been taken to Hospice Haven and was expected to die very soon, so they told me to go, as they knew I would. I sat with Edith as we shared our sorrows. Finally, she insisted that I spend a little time with Jeff before he flew back to D.C... Ricky drove back to Marietta because Julie had stayed behind with Trent, Christie, and Ashley. Dean drove back to Fort Lauderdale. Jeff sat with me for a couple of hours before driving to Gainesville, where he would board a commercial flight to Washington, D.C., on May 12. I joined Edith at Hospice Haven early on the 12th and tried to get her to go home and rest a couple of hours, but she refused. Alvin went home to be with the Lord a little later. We knew that we would be together again very soon.

I started thinking of a way to repay Edith for the surprise. I planned it for her eightieth birthday on April 26, 2016, but a relative arrived at her house way too early. At least everyone seemed to enjoy the time together. Juanita had a stroke about two months later and went home to be with the Lord and Al. Edith and I couldn't decide what to do, so we married on March 18, 2017. Ricky, Julie, Jeff, and Jo came for our wedding at Peace Baptist Church in Branford, Florida. Now Edith and I love each other; we love my children, and they love us. It just keeps getting better! Edith and I took two wonderful cruises and a few other trips, but I had a couple of health issues, so we sold everything in Branford and moved to the Word of Life Bible College RV Park and bought a park model RV, which really isn't an RV. She gave me a fantastic party for my ninetieth birthday on May 14, 2023. I'm straining to try to remember to get even again on April 26, 2026. If we are in Heaven, we will have new bodies, so we will be celebrating better things with the Lord of Lords and King of Kings and waiting to welcome our family and friends.

Marketing & Conclusions – 1990-2025

Ricky has retired from his very successful practice as an oral and maxillofacial surgeon. Julie worked side by side with him as she took care of the family and home. She could have had a good career as a math teacher, but she chose the better course, which ended with a close-knit and loving family. Their children: Trent, Christie, and Ashley have finished college and are well into excellent careers. Joanna has just obtained a master's degree in family healthcare. Her career has spiraled upwards ever since she received a bachelor's degree in the 1990s, beginning with hospitals, hospice management, nursing homes and assisted living management, and much more that is too complicated for a redneck to understand. Her daughter, Olivia, graduated from the University of Virginia the same year Trent graduated with a double degree from the University of Georgia, and Ashley received a bachelor's degree also from UGA, and her twin sister, Christie, graduated from the University of Alabama. Joanna's daughter Alex is still in college. Her son, Benjamin, decided to join the USAF and went through electronics (airborne avionics) school. He is working on aircraft avionics now and has several stripes, but I don't know whether he will make the Air Force a career or get out and go to college on the GI bill like I did. Just hoping he will make the right decision so he will enjoy his job, even if he doesn't get rich. Jeffry has continued after the air charter business, flying for an airline, teaching pilots, etc.. He is now a corporate pilot for a very large auto dealership. I am very proud of my entire family and so happy that their lives are better than mine. I could never love them more. Edith and I are enjoying our twilight time together, especially since the "kids" love us as we love them. We do not need riches! We have much better than gold. About all I can do for God now is to tell others that what He has done for me, He can do for them. Edith is now a witness with me. It took me a long time to realize that God had been in control since I confessed my sins and surrendered to His will in 1958, shortly after my twenty-fifth birthday. He had educated me with excellent knowledge of aircraft, physics, and worldly subjects, but especially in His word. I did not want to travel or leave my family, but He supplied all of my needs to help my family. He put me in places to make money, but never enough to become rich. I was able to witness to people throughout the world, from peasants to nobility. I was only sick one time in my international travels, and that benefited me with five days of rest when I had the flu in Iran. I never feared for my life, but for my people, because I knew that Satan could not touch me while I was in God's will. To summarize: "Everything I did was for God and His Glory. I was only a humble servant. It was none of my business. It's all about Him. To God be the glory. Amen". This was how a redneck rebel traveled from rags to tuxedos.

Addendum: End Times

The rapture of God's church (meaning people of all churches who have accepted Jesus Christ as Savior and Lord) could happen in the twinkling of an eye. All of the signs that He gave us to look for before He appears in the air to call all saints (alive and dead) home have appeared. The false prophet has been in place for a few years, and the antichrist has just been exposed. At this moment, we are entering the Book of Revelation, the last book of the Bible; the King James Version is preferred.

The signs to look for are in 2 Timothy 3:1-5:

In the last days, perilous times shall come.

Men shall be lovers of themselves, covetous, boasters, proud, blasphemers, disobedient to parents, unholy.

Without natural affection, trucebreakers, false accusers, incontinent, fierce, despisers of those that are good.

Traitors, heady, high-minded, lovers of pleasure more than lovers of God.

Having a form of godliness, but denying the power of God.

The False Prophet is identified in Revelation 13 as the great religious leader in the end times who leads people to worship the antichrist. He mimics the Holy Spirit, who leads people to worship Christ. Therefore, the unholy trinity of Satan, antichrist, and false prophet are trying to represent the Holy Trinity of the Father, Son, and Holy Spirit.

Lucifer was the most beautiful and most powerful, and therefore head of the large multitude of angels that God created, perhaps during the six days that He created the heavens and the earth and everything in them. (See the book of Genesis, chapters one and two). Lucifer and one-third of the angels rebelled against God (Isaiah 14:12-17). Then they were cast out of heaven, and Lucifer's name was changed to Satan.

The Bible does not name the Beast, also called antichrist, or false prophet, but provides clues to read and look for. The book of Daniel is a good source of information. All sources are a bit vague because our Lord wanted us to study and be prepared, and during my intense study of end times, I have reached conclusions that I believe to be very clear. I urge you to do your own study before it is too late.

The book of Daniel indicates that the Beast will come out of the old Roman Empire, and the false prophet could be out of the Roman Empire, or he could be a Jew. In my opinion, he came out of Rome. People have always insisted that he was the pope, but I questioned that because radical Islam would never allow the pope to be the head of the "One-World Church" in the last days. However, Pope Francis cleared this up on February 4, 2019, when he signed a joint declaration on human fraternity with Ahmed el-Tayeb in Abu Dhabi, UAE. Headlines stated: "Pope Signs pact with Islam declaring diversity of religions is willed by God". (Credit: Vatican Media).

There have always been false prophets who are here preaching for profit and/or teaching contrary to God's Will. An antichrist has always been around to deny that Christ is

Lord and to mislead everyone possible. The Antichrist is already at work, making friends with everyone and guaranteeing people of all levels and all nations peace and prosperity if they align with him. I backed him for a while until he started all the promises that caused me to recall what I had learned in God's Holy Word.

The rich elite control all governments, including kings and presidents, and they have been working to organize a one-world government with a one-world religion and one-world currency. However, Christ has been holding them up by the Holy Spirit that abides in every Christian. There has been a tremendous number of people turning away from their faith to earn gold and power. Very soon, God the Father will tell Jesus the Son to call His children home, so Jesus will appear in the air and say, "Come Up". Our old bodies will be replaced by eternal Heavenly bodies in a twinkling of an eye, and we will be snatched up to Heaven and be safe and secure forever. Meanwhile, the satanic wealthy elite and their captains, kings, and foot soldiers will be wondering where the Christians went. It's time for all believers to pray up and be ready for the rapture.

Non-believers must get right with Jesus Christ, who gave His life on the cross and shed His blood to cover your sins. Your salvation can be secured by praying to Jesus. Tell Him that you are a sinner and ask Him to forgive you and come into your heart. He is just and will forgive you if you are sincere and will turn away from your sins and follow Him. He knows everything, so you must be sincere.

Photos

Roxie and Quincy Walls

Bill Walls in Cambridge, England

Photos

Bill Walls in Dubai

Jeff

Bill, Edith, Jeff and Ricky

Ricky, Julie, Bill & Edith by the Gulf of Mexico

Photos

Olivia and Alex

Joanna and Ben

www.ingramcontent.com/pod-product-compliance
Lightning Source LLC
Chambersburg PA
CBHW040251090526
44586CB00041B/2752